my kind
of cooking

my kind
of cooking

Mark Sargeant

To Nancy and my daughter Ivy,
the best recipe I have ever made!

First published in Great Britain in 2011 by
Quercus
21 Bloomsbury Square
London
WC1A 2NS

Copyright © Mark Sargeant, 2011

Photography © Emma Lee, 2011 (www.emmaleephotographer.com)

Designed by Ashley Western (www.ash.gb.com)

Recipe for Scrambled eggs 'James Bond' taken from *007 in New York*
Copyright © Ian Fleming 1963

Reprinted with the permission of Ian Fleming Publications Ltd.
www.ianfleming.com

A CIP catalogue record for this book is available
from the British Library

ISBN 978 0 85738 165 1

Printed and bound in Germany

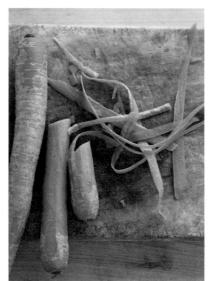

CONTENTS

Introduction

According to my mum, at the age of eight I announced that I wanted to become a chef. From that point on, I continued to surprise people who asked what I wanted to do when I grew up by giving them the same answer: to cook. I sometimes feel that I have never grown up, but I have at least seen my dream through and made good on my early career choice!

For me cooking has always been a passion and it is something I seem to have a natural ability for. At school I wasn't any good at sports or particularly interested in academic work, although this was largely due to boredom. I already knew that I didn't need algebra to be able to cook! The fact that I attended a grammar school with no home economics classes was another reason why my teachers found my career choice strange. When I left school at fifteen to go to catering college, my headmaster told me that I wouldn't amount to anything . . . I should really dedicate this book to him.

I used to watch cookery programmes on television regularly, growing up with Keith Floyd (legend!), Delia Smith, Robert Carrier, Ken Hom and all the other 1980s TV greats. As I started college, the Roux brothers had just had their first series and that was soon to be followed by the programme which changed everything for me. *Marco*, a four-part series consisting of a mental long-haired chef cooking for his mentors, cemented the idea that my chosen profession was absolutely the right one. I never actually ended up working for Marco Pierre White, choosing Gordon Ramsay instead, but Marco was a massive influence on my early career and *White Heat* is still an amazing book.

I went on to work in some truly great restaurants, until 1997, when I made the biggest commitment of my career to date and started working with Gordon at Aubergine. The plan was to stay with him for just one year and then go to France, but somehow it was thirteen years before the time seemed right to 'leave the stable'. I achieved a lot while working with Gordon, from wining a Michelin star at Claridge's to opening three pubs and helping him to write many of his cookery books, as well as working behind (and sometimes in front of) the scenes on many of his TV shows. The thing that remained constant was that I could always be creative, which meant I could develop my passion for food and the diversity that I enjoy so much. I love cooking in service, but that is a very particular style of working, very regimented and precise, especially at Michelin-star level. These days I prefer to experiment, coming up with dishes at a slower pace, and writing a book is the perfect way for me to do this.

So to *My Kind of Cooking*. I must tell you that I am totally honoured and very excited about writing a book of my own. I hope it will be the first of many. My experiences with Gordon's books, even co-publishing one with him, were educational and enjoyable, but this time it is *my* name on the cover. All the recipes within these pages are exactly what the title suggests: dishes that I make at home. As much as I have been inspired by others, I have tried to keep this book as original as possible.

What is *My Kind of Cooking?* I hear you cry. Well, it's anything and everything to do with food really. My passion lies in quality of ingredients and where possible these are always British (I do stray sometimes, but only for the right reasons) and in season. I think that traditional British food is as good as any. But not wanting to limit this book to one style, I have used other influences from around the world, including spices and cooking techniques, allowing you to follow whichever style you wish.

As I get older I find that I am yearning for 'the Good Life' style of living. At the moment this is not really feasible, but one day I will have my house in the country with sheds full of home-made cheese, smoked and cured meats, and with roaming chickens, pigs and so on. One day! For now, though, you will just have to put up with me getting a small part of it out of my system via some of the recipes I have included which are a little slice of that life. Alongside them you will find simplified recipes and techniques from my professional background and the time I have spent in kitchens of the highest standards. All this will give you a real insight into what I love to cook – and I hope you will too.

Tiny morsels
(British tapas)

Spain is famous for its tapas and in most Spanish bars such food is free, enticing you in to drink more! These tiny morsels are delicious, but I think we should be equally proud of some of our own versions. In previous decades there would have been an hors-d'oeuvres section on the menus of hotels and restaurants. Choosing a few items to eat as your starter or as a nibble while you wait for your main meal to be cooked has been transformed into the amuse-bouche we now find in fine-dining restaurants. The recipes that follow are what you would see on an hors-d'oeuvres menu. They also make for great snacks to accompany drinks, as they are not only full of flavour but sometimes lovely and salty, the perfect combination with a few pints or some chilled bubbles. The danger here is that they are all so delicious and moreish you may end up eating too many, leaving no room for anything else!

Dates in duvets

Chipolatas with Lea & Perrins glaze

Crispy quail's eggs with celery salt mayonnaise

Radishes with salty anchovy sauce

Fried chestnut mushrooms with Stichleton dip

Smoked haddock and curry Scotch egg

Broad beans on toast

Almond potatoes

Spicy cheese puffs

Read's cheese on toast

Dates in duvets

SERVES 4

16 best-quality dates (such as
Medjool)

16 large whole almonds (fresh
if possible)

16 rashers of organic smoked
streaky bacon

olive oil for frying

3 tbsp sherry vinegar

This is really a posh version of Pigs in Blankets and
much more luxurious. Dates are very sweet and
have a caramel-like flavour, so the sherry vinegar
glaze helps to cut the sweetness.

Carefully remove the stones from the dates, which should be
easy if they're nice and soft, then replace each stone with an
almond, simply pushing it into the hole left by the stone. Next
you need to wrap each date in a slice of bacon, leaving a spiral
pattern at the top of the date. The bacon will wrap around more
than once, but don't worry as this helps to keep the shape.

Once all the dates are wrapped up, place them in the fridge for
about 10 minutes – this will stop the bacon unravelling during
cooking. Heat some oil in a frying pan and pack the dates in as
close together as possible so the bacon doesn't fall off. Gently
fry them, turning carefully on a regular basis until the bacon
is golden and slightly crispy. Pour off any excess fat, then
allow the pan to cool slightly before adding the sherry vinegar.
Reduce the vinegar until it glazes the dates, then serve.

Chipolatas
with Lea & Perrins glaze

SERVES 4

olive oil

16 good-quality chipolatas

1 clove of garlic, peeled and crushed

1 sprig of fresh thyme, leaves only

1 tbsp soy sauce

1 tbsp Lea & Perrins

2 or 3 (or lots of) drops of Tabasco Sauce

I love these little snacks, especially with a few drinks. The idea is a British spin on the Spanish warm chorizo sausage in the tapas bar. I've simply replaced the chorizo with a good-quality chipolata and then spiced it up with a generous glug of Lea & Perrins. I like mine very spicy, but it's up to you how far you go.

Add just a few drops of olive oil to a good non-stick pan and heat gently. Fry the chipolatas in the oil slowly for approximately 10–12 minutes, turning them frequently so that they get an all-over even golden colour and making sure they are thoroughly cooked through. Remove them from the pan and drain on some kitchen paper, then pour off the fat and wipe the pan (this is important so that you don't get a greasy finished product).

Place the chipolatas back in the pan and add all the other ingredients. Cook over a low heat so that the liquid reduces slowly, as this imparts more flavour and gives a better glaze. When the liquid is syrupy and the chipolatas are coated in a dark spicy glaze they're ready to serve. Try not to eat them all before you put them in a serving bowl!

Crispy quail's eggs
with celery salt mayonnaise

Another twist on a classic. Quail's eggs, or gull's eggs in season, are delicious just boiled and peeled, then dipped in celery salt, but I wanted to do something different. Once deep-fried, the crispy breadcrumbs add lovely texture and the celery salt gives great flavour to the mayonnaise.

Make sure that the quail's eggs are at room temperature first, as this prevents them from cracking. Bring a large pan of salted water to the boil and lower in the eggs gently. Simmer them for 2 minutes and 11 seconds (!), which is the perfect time if you want a soft yolk. Plunge the eggs immediately into iced water and leave to cool. Meanwhile mix the celery salt into the mayonnaise and check the seasoning – it needs to be on the salty side.

When the eggs are cool, shell them and rinse under cold water to ensure there are no little bits of shell attached, then dry on kitchen paper. Roll them first in a saucer of seasoned flour, then in the beaten egg and finally in the breadcrumbs. In a pan suitable for deep-frying, heat the vegetable oil to about 180°C. If you don't have a thermometer, test by sprinkling breadcrumbs, and when they sizzle it's ready. Lower the eggs into the oil very carefully and fry until golden brown and crispy. Drain on kitchen paper, season with sea salt and dip away!

SERVES 4

16 quail's eggs
1 tsp celery salt
5 tbsp English mustard mayonnaise (see page 236)
3 tbsp seasoned flour
1 large egg, beaten
a handful of fresh breadcrumbs
vegetable oil for deep-frying
sea salt

Radishes
with salty anchovy sauce

SERVES 4

20 radishes (such as French
Breakfast)

1 clove of garlic, peeled

50g salted anchovies in oil,
drained

1–2 tsp red wine vinegar

sea salt

125g English mustard
mayonnaise (see page 236)

Early spring brings some amazing vegetables and I
love it when the new-season radishes arrive. Large
and slightly sweeter than usual, they are the perfect
vessel for dipping into this rich salty anchovy sauce.
Crunchy and delicious.

Trim the green stalk of the radishes, leaving a little to hold on
to, then wash them well in cold water and pat dry. Place in
the fridge to maintain crispness. Using a pestle and mortar,
pound the garlic, anchovies, vinegar and a pinch of sea salt to
a smooth paste and whisk into the mayonnaise. Remove the
radishes from the fridge and serve with the sauce immediately.

Fried chestnut mushrooms
with Stichleton dip

SERVES 4

16 even-sized chestnut mushrooms, trimmed and cleaned

3 tbsp seasoned flour

1 large free-range egg, beaten

a handful of fresh breadcrumbs

250ml double cream

1 bay leaf

freshly ground black pepper

100g Stichleton cheese, crumbled

vegetable oil for deep-frying

As a boy, I used to work in a steak house and I'm ashamed to say I served up many a substandard fried mushroom with a blue cheese dip. This is a much nicer version and if you haven't tried Stichleton yet, then I urge you to. Made in the same way as Stilton, it has a much softer, creamier texture.

Coat the mushrooms first in the flour, then in the egg and finally in the breadcrumbs. Set aside. Heat the cream along with the bay leaf and a couple of grinds of black pepper until just under boiling, then slowly whisk in the crumbled cheese until it's melted and the sauce has a creamy texture. Remove the bay leaf and keep the sauce warm.

Heat the vegetable oil to 180°C (if you don't have a thermometer, test by sprinkling breadcrumbs, and when they sizzle it's ready) and carefully fry the mushrooms until they are crispy and golden brown, then drain on kitchen paper. Serve the crispy mushrooms with cocktail sticks and the warm, creamy sauce on the side. Mmmmmmm!

Smoked haddock and curry Scotch egg

My version of a Scotch egg owes something to Italian arancini, but the curry powder adds that British 'Coronation' feel which I adore. It is quite a long process, but I promise you the work will be worth it when you take your first bite.

Place the 4 eggs in a saucepan and add enough cold water to cover them by about a centimetre. Bring the water up to simmering point and leave the eggs for 6 minutes, then remove and cool them under cold running water. Carefully remove their shells and refrigerate them while you make the haddock rice.

Place the haddock in a saucepan with the chicken stock and bay leaves, and poach for about 5 minutes. Remove from the heat and allow to cool, then carefully remove the haddock and bay leaves, retaining the stock for the rice. Strain the stock into a jug or clean pan. Remove the skin from the haddock and flake it into large pieces before setting them aside. In a larger pan melt the butter and sweat the chopped onion until soft, then add the curry powder and cook for a couple of minutes to release the flavours. Stir in the rice so that it becomes completely coated in the butter, onion and curry powder mixture, then start to add the stock. As this is not a risotto and will be cooked for longer, it is OK to add the stock in about three lots and boil it fairly quickly. By the time all the stock has been absorbed, the mixture should be fairly thick, which is perfect. This will take approximately 15–20 minutes. Now stir in the coriander, Parmesan and haddock. Season with a little sea salt and black pepper, then tip out on to a tray lined with cling film and leave to cool. When the rice has cooled completely, it will be firm but malleable. Carefully mould it around the eggs, shaping it with your hands to encase each one.

When the eggs are completely covered dust them in flour, then dip them in beaten egg and finally breadcrumbs. They should now look like rather odd-shaped tennis balls. Heat your oil to 180°C (see recipe opposite) and fry the eggs for approximately 2 minutes until they are a lovely golden brown. They can be eaten like this, but if you want them to be warm all the way through, then pop them in a moderate oven for a few minutes.

SERVES 4

- 4 eggs (Burford Browns are perfect for this dish)
- 100g undyed smoked haddock
- 500ml white chicken stock (see page 239), plus more if necessary
- 2 bay leaves
- 50g salted butter
- 1 onion, peeled and finely chopped
- 1–2 tsp curry powder
- 80g Carnaroli risotto rice
- 1 tbsp fresh coriander, chopped
- 40g Parmesan cheese, freshly grated
- sea salt and freshly ground black pepper
- 1 tbsp seasoned flour
- 1 large free-range egg, beaten
- 50g fresh white breadcrumbs
- vegetable oil for deep-frying

Broad beans on toast

SERVES 4

400g podded broad beans
(frozen are good)

30g salted butter

1 clove of garlic, peeled and
crushed

250ml double cream

1–2 tbsp fresh flat-leaf parsley,
leaves only, chopped

sea salt and freshly ground
black pepper

4 slices of sourdough bread

olive oil

My mum used to serve these beans as a vegetable, but when I was young I hated the smell of broad beans. Now I'm all grown up I love them! I keep the beans in their skins, but by all means peel them if you have time on your hands. The fresh taste goes perfectly with the charred, crunchy bread.

Heat plenty of salted water in a large saucepan. When it comes to the boil, add the broad beans, turn down the heat and simmer for 6–8 minutes, until tender. Drain the beans in a colander and refresh them by rinsing under cold running water.

Then heat the butter in a wide, heavy-bottomed frying pan with the garlic, add the beans and cook over a low heat for 2 minutes, stirring gently. Add the double cream and cook uncovered over a moderate heat for 3–4 minutes, until it thickens and coats the beans. Add the chopped parsley and season well, especially with black pepper, then set aside.

Heat the grill pan until it is smoking. Drizzle the slices of bread with a generous glug of olive oil and a good sprinkle of sea salt, then grill them well until slightly burned around the edges. Place a slice of bread on a plate and spoon on the creamed beans. If you want you can drizzle over a bit more oil, but I prefer just to tuck straight in!

Almond potatoes

MAKES APPROX. 20 BALLS

400g potatoes, peeled and cut into equal-sized pieces

sea salt

freshly grated nutmeg

10g salted butter

125ml whole milk

1 large free-range egg yolk

40g plain flour, plus extra for coating

1 large free-range egg, beaten

100g flaked almonds

vegetable oil for deep-frying

My very first job in London was at Boodle's gentlemen's club and it was fantastic training. The head chef, Keith Podmore, was a great teacher and a hard but fair taskmaster. These are tricky to get right, as you need to make sure that the potatoes are nice and dry before you fry them. I found this out the hard way through the wrath of Keith.

Place the potatoes in a pan of cold salted water and bring to the boil, then reduce the heat and simmer gently for 10–12 minutes, until the potatoes are tender. Drain and let them sit for a couple of minutes so the excess water can evaporate. Add a generous pinch of salt, a grating of nutmeg and the butter, then start mashing.

Slowly add the milk and keep mashing until the mixture becomes very smooth and creamy: you want a fairly stiff mash. Add the egg yolk and carry on mashing. As the mixture turns sticky, slowly add the flour until it firms up. Now use it to form potato balls, which you put on a plate before leaving them in the fridge for 30 minutes.

Take the pre-formed croquettes out of the fridge and, yes, you've guessed it, coat them in flour, then beaten egg . . . but wait, instead of breadcrumbs use the flaked almonds! Next, heat your oil to 180°C (if you don't have a thermometer, test by sprinkling breadcrumbs, and when they sizzle it's ready) and deep-fry the croquettes for about 2 minutes, by which time they should be golden brown. If not, give them another minute or so until you have the right colour. Take them out and drain on kitchen paper. Season with sea salt and serve piping hot.

Spicy cheese puffs

These are the perfect warm treat to have with a nice cold glass of champagne. Get good-quality Parmesan for this, as you can really taste the difference. I make mine nice and spicy with the addition of cayenne pepper, but for something different try smoked paprika. A good tip here is to double your mix because these are seriously moreish!

Preheat the oven to 220°C/gas mark 7 and line a baking sheet with parchment paper.

Heat 125ml of water in a saucepan with the butter, salt and cayenne pepper until the butter has melted. Add the flour all at once and stir vigorously until the mixture pulls away from the sides into a smooth ball. Remove from the heat and allow to rest for 2 minutes. Add the eggs, one at a time, stirring quickly to make sure they don't cook. The mixture will appear lumpy at first, but after a minute or so it will smooth out. Add about three-quarters of the Parmesan, the cayenne pepper and the chives and stir until well mixed.

Scrape the mixture into a pastry bag fitted with a wide plain tip and pipe the dough into evenly spaced mounds on the baking sheet, making each about the size of a small cherry tomato. Top each puff with a bit of the remaining cheese before putting the baking sheet into the oven. Bake for 10 minutes, then turn the oven down to 190°C/gas mark 5 and bake for an additional 15–20 minutes, until the puffs are golden brown. Remove and eat straight away.

MAKES APPROX. 26 PUFFS

40g salted butter, cut into cubes

sea salt and freshly ground black pepper

a generous pinch of cayenne pepper

70g flour

2 large free-range eggs

90g Parmesan cheese, freshly grated

a bunch of fresh chives, finely chopped

Read's cheese on toast

SERVES 4 (MAKES APPROX.
16 SLICES)

110g cream cheese

110g Cheddar cheese, grated
(a nice strong one like
Montgomery is perfect)

2 large free-range egg yolks

sea salt and freshly ground
black pepper

2–3 tbsp fresh chives, finely
chopped

1 thin baguette, cut into slices

This recipe is another tribute to a restaurant
that featured heavily in my training. Read's in
Faversham, Kent, is run by Rona and David Pitchford
and I worked there for three years. David is what
I would call a true mentor and I love them both
like family. This simple but tasty little snack is still
served there as a pre-dinner nibble.

Mix the cream cheese in a large bowl to soften and smooth
it, then add the grated cheese and egg yolks. Season well,
especially with black pepper, add the chives and give things
a really good mix – you want the chives to bruise slightly and
release all of their oniony flavour. Chill in the fridge for about
10 minutes.

Toast the baguette. When the toast has cooled, mound the
cheese on top and cook under a very hot grill until the cheese is
golden and bubbling.

Starters' orders

Some people say that the way you start and end your meal is the most important factor in determining how much you enjoy it, which doesn't say much for the poor old main course. This is, of course, not true, as each course is as important as the next, but there is definitely something to be said for starting as you mean to go on, and these dishes will not disappoint. As this book is not about three-course meals, a lot of the recipes in this chapter will make good light lunch or brunch dishes as well as being a wonderful way to start a meal.

Omelette 'Gordon Bennett'

SERVES 2

1 tsp plain flour

15g salted butter at room temperature, plus extra for frying

200ml whole milk

1 bay leaf

¼ tsp black peppercorns

1 slice of onion, peeled

200g undyed kipper fillet

2 large free-range egg yolks

1 tbsp single cream

30g mature Cheddar cheese, finely grated

sea salt and freshly ground black pepper

4 large free-range eggs

We all know the famous omelette 'Arnold Bennett', so here is my version but done slightly differently. My grandad Ted used to say 'Gordon Bennett' all the time and had kippers for breakfast every Sunday. So, in a tribute to Ted boy, I have replaced the usual smoked haddock with kippers and it works really well.

Blend the flour and butter together to make a paste, then chill in the fridge until firm. Meanwhile pour the milk into a small pan, add the bay leaf, peppercorns and onion, and heat gently to just below boiling point. Lower in the kipper, skin-side down, then cover with a piece of greaseproof paper and poach gently for about 4 minutes, until the fish is just beginning to show signs of flaking when pressed. Remove the fish from the milk with a slotted spoon and, when it is cool enough to handle, remove the skin and any bones and flake into small pieces. Strain the milk into a bowl and discard the aromatics. Pour 100ml of the infused milk into a clean small pan and return to the heat. Gradually whisk in the butter paste, adding small pieces at a time, and bring to the boil. Cook for 1–2 minutes, whisking constantly until you have a smooth sauce. Put the egg yolks in a bowl and beat lightly with the cream. Gradually whisk in the sauce, then fold in the kipper and half of the cheese. Check for seasoning.

Preheat the grill to a medium setting. Place an omelette pan over a medium to high heat. Break the eggs into a bowl, season and beat with a fork. Add a knob of butter to the pan and swirl it about to coat. When the butter starts to foam, pour in the eggs. Stir them continually, tilting the pan from side to side, until the eggs set on the bottom and the top is soft and creamy. Remove the pan from the heat and pour the kipper mixture on top of the omelette. Sprinkle over the remaining cheese and grill for a few minutes until golden brown.

Devilled chicken liver and tarragon vol au vents

Anything 'devilled' ticks my box and chicken livers are something I feel we don't use enough of. Most people would make a pâté out of them but rarely eat them on their own, so this recipe is a must. Tarragon is the perfect herb for this dish and the crunchy, buttery puff pastry soaks up all the sauce. Really, really delicious.

Preheat the oven to 200°C/gas mark 6.

To make the vol au vent cases, roll out the pastry until it is about 20mm thick. Use a fluted cutter to cut four discs roughly 7.5cm in diameter. With a 5cm cutter, mark smaller circles inside each of the discs, but don't go all the way through the pastry. Brush the pastry with beaten egg, then bake for about 15 minutes, until puffed and golden brown. Carefully remove and reserve the inner discs of pastry so you are left with crisp pastry cases, then put the cases back into the oven for 2 minutes to dry out. Set aside for later.

Trim the chicken livers, dry them on kitchen paper and cut any large pieces in half. Mix together the paprika, cayenne pepper, Tabasco, mustard, Lea & Perrins and ketchup in a bowl. Add the livers and toss to coat. Heat up a large non-stick frying pan and add the oil. When the pan is very hot, add the livers and marinade, season with salt and sauté for 1 minute on each side. Pour in the Madeira and cook for 2 minutes. Add the cream, bring to the boil and cook for a further minute. Stir in the tarragon and add a few tablespoons of water if the sauce is a bit thick. Serve in the pastry cases and pop a lid on top of each.

SERVES 4

500g packet of all-butter puff pastry
1 large free-range egg, beaten
500g chicken livers
1 tsp paprika
½ tsp cayenne pepper
a few dashes of Tabasco Sauce
2 tsp English mustard
2 tsp Lea & Perrins
1 heaped tbsp tomato ketchup
2 tsp olive oil
sea salt
50ml Madeira
80–100ml double cream
1 tbsp fresh tarragon, chopped

Potted Brixham crab
with harissa

I adore crab and would eat it every day if I could. It beats lobster hands down in my eyes. My heart lies in British food, but I think this means the product that you use and not the recipe, so here I have combined the classic method of potting with the Middle Eastern chilli paste harissa. Usually you would spice up the brown meat with Tabasco and Lea & Perrins, so this works really well.

Check the crab meat for any bits of shell and cartilage, then wrap with cling film and chill in the fridge.

Put the shallot, sherry and a grating of nutmeg in a small saucepan and season well. Bring to the boil and let it bubble vigorously for about 2 minutes, until the liquid has reduced by half, then whisk in the butter. Leave it to simmer very gently for a few minutes. Remove the pan from the heat and let the flavours infuse as the butter cools. Pour the butter mixture into a fine sieve set over a measuring jug and press down to extract the juice from the shallots. Discard the solids.

Mix the crab meat with the Lea and Perrins, lemon juice, butter mixture and harissa. Season to taste, then spoon into the ramekins, cover with cling film and chill in the fridge for 2–3 hours, until set. Remove 30 minutes before you are ready to eat. Serve the potted crab with buttered brown toast and lemon wedges.

FILLS 4 LARGE (100ML) RAMEKINS

200g white crab meat (Brixham crabs are great)

100g brown crab meat

1 banana shallot, peeled and finely chopped

4 tbsp sherry

freshly grated nutmeg

sea salt and freshly ground black pepper

175g unsalted butter, cut into cubes

1½ tsp Lea & Perrins

a squeeze of lemon juice, according to taste

1 tbsp harissa paste

Leftover roast chicken soup
with toasted breadcrumbs

SERVES 4

1 tbsp olive oil

2 onions, peeled and chopped

1 clove of garlic, peeled and crushed

3 medium carrots, peeled and chopped

1 tbsp fresh thyme leaves, roughly chopped

1.4 litres white chicken stock (see page 239)

300g leftover roast chicken, skin removed and shredded

200g frozen peas

sea salt and freshly ground black pepper

3 tbsp double cream

the zest and juice of 1 lemon

a knob of salted butter

200g fresh breadcrumbs

Most people end up with a chicken carcass and probably some meat after a roast. Some might think of making a stock out of it, but take that stock a stage further and you have the most amazing soup. It's rich and velvety and has an incredible depth of flavour. As the old saying goes, 'You can just feel it doing you good.' The lemon zest really enhances the taste and the toasted breadcrumbs give a nod to the classic roast garnish.

Heat the olive oil in a large heavy-based pan. Add the onions, garlic, carrots and thyme, and fry gently for 15 minutes. Stir in the stock and bring to the boil, then cover and simmer for 10 minutes. Add the chicken, then remove half the mixture and purée in a liquidizer. Tip this back into the pan with the rest of the soup, peas and seasoning. Simmer for 5 minutes, until warmed through. Mix in the cream and the lemon zest and juice. Keep the soup warm, but do not let it boil.

In a frying pan melt the butter and let it brown slightly. Add the breadcrumbs and cook over a medium heat until they are nicely toasted and nutty brown, then drain on kitchen paper. Pour the soup into bowls, sprinkle over the breadcrumbs and dig in.

Scrambled eggs 'James Bond'

FOR FOUR SYBARITES

12 newly laid eggs
salt and pepper
6oz sweet dairy butter
chives

I LOVE JAMES BOND. In fact I wish I *was* James Bond, and I make no qualms about it! But now that's out of the way I will explain that, while I enjoy the films, I love Ian Fleming's ability to take readers on such a wonderful gastronomic journey through the narrative in his books. The way in which he describes the atmosphere of the dining rooms, and the food and drinks that go with them, is the best part for me, and I sometimes find myself drooling as I turn the pages. I came across this recipe as I was reading probably the shortest of all the Bond short stories: *007 in New York*. It is actually written as a recipe, with method and all! So here it is, unchanged, and for your pleasure as much as mine.

Break the eggs into a bowl. Beat thoroughly with a fork and season well. In a small copper or heavy bottomed saucepan melt four ounces of the butter. When melted, pour in the eggs and cook over a very low heat, whisking continuously with a small egg whisk. While the eggs are slightly more moist than you would wish for eating, remove the pan from the heat, add the rest of the butter and continue whisking for 30 seconds, adding the chopped chives or *fines herbes*. Serve moist on hot buttered toast (the crusts trimmed off, of course) in individual copper dishes (for appearance only) with pink champagne (Taittinger) and low music.

Bloody brilliant!

Home-made corned beef, watercress and dill pickle salad

If you decide to make corned beef specially for this dish I doff my cap to you, but it's more likely that you'll be using leftovers from the salt beef recipe on page 116. I love this salad as it has so many elements to it: salty, peppery, vinegary and, believe it or not, healthy. The corned beef is not to be confused with, or even replaced by, the tinned variety, as that has a completely different flavour – although I would, of course, use tinned corned beef for a pie or indeed a lovely fried hash.

Pull the salt beef into thick strands (this is easier to do if the beef is at room temperature) and set aside. To make the dressing, put the vinegar, mustard, garlic, lemon zest and juice and oil into a bowl and whisk to emulsify. Add the beef to the dressing and coat well, then leave to steep for a minute or so. Add the radishes, dill pickles and watercress and toss gently. Pile on to plates, season well with black pepper and just a touch of sea salt, then dig in!

SERVES 4

250g cooked salt beef (see page 116)

2 tbsp cider vinegar

2 tsp English mustard

1 clove of garlic, peeled and crushed

the zest of 1 and the juice of ½ a lemon

6 tbsp olive oil

10 radishes, thinly sliced

2 large dill pickles, thinly sliced

100g young, peppery watercress, picked and cleaned

sea salt and freshly ground black pepper

British snails
with parsley pearl barley

SERVES 4

olive oil

1 medium onion, peeled and
finely chopped

2 cloves of garlic, peeled and
finely chopped

1 sprig of fresh thyme, leaves
only

175g pearl barley

750ml hot white chicken stock
(see page 239)

6 tbsp fresh flat-leaf parsley,
leaves only, chopped

24 cooked snails (Helen
Howard from Slow and Grow
in Kent does the best)

50g salted butter

a squeeze of lemon juice

sea salt and freshly ground
black pepper

We think of snails as French food, and indeed it was the French who brought the delights of a very garlicky snail to our table, but as the British market came to love them, so British snail farms quickly grew. Being the proud patriot that I am, I will of course now say that our home-grown snails taste as good, if not better, than their French counterparts. So why not take a leap of faith, try them and make up your own minds?

Heat a glug of olive oil in a medium pan over a medium-low heat. Add the onion, one clove of garlic and the thyme leaves and cook gently, stirring occasionally, for 6–8 minutes, until softened. Add the pearl barley and cook for 1 minute to coat the grains in oil. Add a quarter of the stock to the pan and simmer, stirring occasionally, until it has all has been absorbed. Add another quarter of the stock and continue in this way until all the stock is absorbed – it should take about 40 minutes for the barley to be tender but still a little firm. Add 5 tablespoons of the parsley and set aside to keep warm.

In a frying pan melt the butter and let it brown slightly. Throw in the snails and swirl them round in the pan to warm through, before adding the remaining clove of garlic, parsley and lemon juice. Season well, then divide the pearl barley between four plates, top with the snails and drizzle over the buttery juices.

Brunch salad
with Burford Brown egg

If you want to go for a 'feel good about yourself' lighter option while still enjoying all the brunch trimmings, this dish is for you. As usual it is about good ingredients, making sure that you have the best-quality bacon, preferably home-cured, and very fresh eggs. I adore Burford Browns and these days you can get them in any supermarket, so there is no excuse not to try them! They are how eggs used to be, with a large velvety orange yolk, and can even come adorned with the odd feather. I used to live near an old barn shop, which meant that getting fresh eggs was the norm. I miss those days and am sad they will never return. But Burford Browns are the very best alternative.

Carefully coat the poached eggs twice in flour, then beaten egg and finally breadcrumbs. Set aside in the fridge.

In a non-stick pan heat a little olive oil and fry the bacon until crispy. Remove and drain on kitchen paper. In the remaining bacon fat cook the black pudding and keep warm. Fry the slices of bread in the same pan, adding a little more oil as necessary until golden, then remove from the pan. Add the onion slices to the pan and caramelize in olive oil, then deglaze with 2 tablespoons of sherry vinegar and set aside.

To serve each person, place the fried bread in the centre of a warm bowl and top with some onions. Place the black pudding on top of the onions. Deep-fry the eggs in hot vegetable oil (180°C) for 15–30 seconds, until crisp and golden, then drain on kitchen paper before placing them on the black pudding. Mix the salad leaves and toss them in the remaining sherry vinegar, then scatter them round the black pudding and eggs. Finally, add the crispy bacon on top of the salad. In the summer you can add slow-cooked cherry tomatoes to the dish.

SERVES 4

4 Burford Brown eggs, poached, then cooled in iced water and drained

flour for coating

1 large free-range egg, beaten

fresh breadcrumbs for coating

olive oil

8 thick rashers of bacon, cut into lardons

4 large slices of black pudding

4 slices of white country bread

2 onions, peeled and thinly sliced

3 tbsp sherry vinegar

vegetable oil for deep-frying

1 head of frisée lettuce

1 punnet of pea shoots

1 punnet of coriander cress

Fennel, red onion, orange, parsley and goat's cheese salad

SERVES 4

2 fennel bulbs

1 red onion, peeled and thinly sliced

2 oranges

a big handful of fresh flat-leaf parsley, leaves only

2 tbsp olive oil

sea salt and freshly ground black pepper

200g good-quality soft goat's cheese

Good food is a mixture of key things – basically flavour, texture, aroma and colour. This salad encompasses all of these. It is visually stunning, but most importantly tastes fresh and delicious. Putting the fennel in iced water makes it ultra crispy and washing the onion helps to get maximum flavour without the nose-stinging twang that raw onion can have. The orange gives a sweet, fruity note and it is all brought together with a soft, creamy goat's cheese. This will also make a great main course if you super-size it.

Remove the tough outer parts of the fennel and cut off the shoots that stick out at the top, reserving the green fronds (they look a bit like dill). Slice off the root end at the bottom. Quarter the fennel bulbs, wash thoroughly and slice very finely. You can use a sharp knife, a Japanese mandolin or a food processor to do this. Put the fennel in a bowl of iced water and leave to soak for about 20 minutes so that it goes really crisp. Drain when needed and dry on a clean cloth. Now rinse the red onion slices under a cold tap for a few minutes, which crisps them up but also gets rid of the strong juices, making the onion more palatable. Leave to drain.

Next, finely grate the zest and squeeze the juice from half an orange. Remove the skin and the white pith from the rest of the oranges, then cut the orange segments away between the inner sectioning membranes over a bowl to catch the juices. Now tear the parsley leaves roughly by hand. Make a dressing with the orange zest and juice, olive oil, salt and pepper. Toss fennel slices and fronds, red onion slices, orange segments and torn parsley in the dressing and divide between four bowls, then break the goat's cheese over the top. Season with an extra grind of black pepper and serve.

Warm mixed tomato, shallot and Thai basil salad

SERVES 4

12 tomatoes, a variety of colours if possible

sea salt and freshly ground black pepper

3 tbsp extra virgin olive oil

2 cloves of garlic, peeled and finely minced

2 banana shallots, peeled and sliced into rings

1 tbsp fresh flat-leaf parsley, leaves only, chopped

1 tbsp fresh Thai basil, chopped

2 tbsp red wine vinegar

Everyone loves a simple tomato salad and this is a sexier version of the classic. I was working at Borough Market one day in early June and popped across to Turnips vegetable stand, where I was confronted with the most amazing selection of tomatoes I have ever seen. There were so many different shapes, sizes and colours, some of which I had never seen before. Fred, the owner, told me that the Italians only use red tomatoes for sauces and insist on green ones for salads. For this recipe, I would urge you to go to your local market and choose as many different types as they have.

Cut the cores from the tomatoes, then slice each of them into 8 to 10 wedges and put in a bowl. Season with salt and pepper and drizzle with a little oil. Heat a large non-stick pan, add the tomatoes and toss them over the heat for no more than 1 minute. Once the tomatoes are just warm (you don't want to cook them), place them back in the bowl. Combine with the remaining ingredients and toss to blend well. Serve with crusty bread on the side.

Smoked and cured fish

In an ideal world I would love to make everything myself, including smoking my own fish. While this is possible to do at home and can be very satisfying, to get perfect results takes time, practice and of course a smokehouse! So, for those of you who are clever enough and have the space, why not enjoy yourself and the rewards of your labours? Curing fish, on the other hand, is much more straightforward and the results are always delicious. In this chapter there are some great recipes for fish prepared both ways.

Lime and sesame cured sea bream

SERVES 4

4 large sea bream fillets (about 250g each)

the juice of 4 limes and 1 lemon

1 red chilli, deseeded (if you don't want it too hot) and thinly sliced

a knob of fresh ginger, peeled and grated

2 tbsp sesame oil

sea salt and freshly ground black pepper

a pinch of caster sugar

1 tbsp fresh coriander, chopped

4 spring onions, sliced

Sea bream is one of my favourite fish. It has a lovely sweet flavour and can be roasted, baked, steamed or poached, and, as in this recipe, is fantastic eaten raw. This is a ceviche-style dish, which calls for ultra-fresh fish, otherwise the end result is nowhere near as good. While this method of curing has its origins in Latin America, I like to give it a bit of an Asian feel, so it's really a cross between a ceviche and sashimi.

Ask your fishmonger to fillet, skin and pin-bone the fish for you. Slice the fillets across the grain into pieces 1cm thick and lay them flat on serving plates. Chill the fish in the fridge while you make the dressing. Mix the citrus juice, chilli, ginger and sesame oil in a bowl and season to taste. Add a little pinch of sugar if you find it too sharp, but I like it without!

Pour the dressing over the fish and leave to marinate for 30 minutes or so, then sprinkle over the coriander and spring onions and serve. There may be dressing left over, in which case it'll keep in the fridge for a few days.

Smoked trout and horseradish pâté

When I have dinner parties at home I always make a smoked fish pâté to spread on toast to have as a canapé, or nibble with a glass of champagne before the main event. This works as a starter more than just a canapé really, which gives you more time to be with your guests – or, like me, to hide in the kitchen with a decent bottle of wine pretending to cook! Other smoked fish works equally well with this recipe, particularly mackerel and salmon, and if this is a special occasion you could use all three.

Skin the smoked trout and remove all the bones. Roughly flake the fillets into the bowl of a food processor and add the butter, lemon zest and juice, horseradish, cayenne pepper and lots of black pepper. Mix to a rough paste, then pour in the crème fraîche and pulse again.

Add the chives and stir well to combine. Check the seasoning, adding more lemon juice if required. Place in a serving bowl with a large handful of watercress and wedges of lemon on the side. Serve with crusty bread or toast if you prefer.

MAKES APPROX. 450G

225g smoked trout fillets

110g unsalted butter, softened

the zest and juice of ½ lemon

1–2 tbsp hot creamed horseradish

a large pinch of cayenne pepper

freshly ground black pepper

125g crème fraîche

2 tbsp fresh chives, chopped

a bunch of picked, cleaned watercress

1 lemon, cut into wedges

Kippers
with fondant potatoes

SERVES 4

1kg potatoes (Desiree are the best), peeled

50g salted butter

200ml white chicken (see page 239) or vegetable stock (see page 240)

1 clove of garlic, peeled

1 sprig of fresh thyme, leaves only, chopped

sea salt and freshly ground black pepper

4 excellent-quality undyed kippers

olive oil

In 1987, when Marco Pierre White was at the height of his culinary career, I was lucky enough to eat at his restaurant Harvey's. I was still studying at college, the meal blew me away and Marco was to be my hero for the next few years. This was the first time I had eaten butter fondant potatoes, which I thought were the most amazing things I had ever tasted in my life. I spent the following day at home trying to make them until I got them right – which, without instruction, was a difficult if worthy task! Using them as a base for smoked kippers, I presented this dish to my mum as an original and wonderful meal. I was only seventeen and thought there and then that I deserved three Michelin stars.

Preheat the grill.

Cut the potatoes into even-sized pieces: rough 2cm cubes are perfect for this dish, but normally you would do them in big barrel shapes. In a large sauté pan melt the butter over a low heat, add the potatoes and cook slowly, shaking the pan and stirring regularly until they are golden brown all over. This will take 10 minutes. Add 100ml of the stock and simmer for roughly 5 minutes. Add the remaining stock, garlic and thyme and cook for 10 minutes, until the stock has reduced and potatoes are tender. Remove from the heat, season and keep warm.

Place the kippers on an ovenproof tray and drizzle with a little olive oil, then grill them (without turning) for approximately 5–7 minutes. Spoon any juices from the kippers over the potatoes before placing them on a warm plate. Top with the fish.

Broccoli goes very well with this dish, but I like it as it is, or even with some bread and butter. Rich but fantastic!

Smoked eel and celeriac soup

SERVES 4

50g salted butter

500g celeriac, peeled and cut into small cubes

2 large shallots, peeled and sliced

bones, head and trimmings from 1 large smoked eel

150ml white wine

1 litre hot white chicken stock (see page 239)

75ml double cream

sea salt and freshly ground black pepper

After researching eels, I came to realize that what I used to consider the rats of the river were actually impressive creatures that undertake an amazingly lengthy journey to spawn in the Sargasso Sea. This inspired a new-found enthusiasm for the eel in me. This soup is a good way to use up every last part of a smoked eel, as it's the bones and any trimmings you need (you may have to order them from your fishmonger). It tastes amazing, so savour every mouthful.

Heat the butter in a large pan over a medium heat. Add the celeriac and shallots and sweat them gently for about 10 minutes to soften without browning. Add the eel bones and the white wine, bring to the boil and reduce the liquid by half. Add the chicken stock and bring to the boil. Reduce the heat and simmer for about 5 minutes to reduce the liquid by half and until the celeriac is tender. Remove from the heat and take out the head before transferring the soup to a food processor and blending until smooth. Pass the soup through a fine sieve back into the saucepan, as this will remove any bits of bone that haven't been puréed, then add the cream and heat through. Season to taste and serve in warm bowls or mugs.

This recipe is designed to use up every last bit of the eel, but if you have any flesh left add some to the soup at the end and warm through gently.

Smoked cod's roe and crème fraîche
(a quick tarama)

These days we all love snacking on flat breads with hummus and taramasalata, but rarely do we consider making them ourselves. Usually, making a real tarama can be quite time-consuming, but this recipe is quick and tastes delicious. You may need to search quite hard to find smoked cod's roe, but some fishmongers and delis will sell it. It is an ingredient I urge you to try.

Soak the bread in warm water for about 5 minutes, then squeeze it out well. You need to use sourdough for this recipe as it has a good firm texture; normal bread would just disintegrate and be too soggy. Place the bread in a food processor with the cod's roe and garlic and purée to a smooth paste. Add the crème fraîche, lemon juice and olive oil, then mix again until smooth. Season with black pepper only, as the roe is already very salty. Serve in a bowl with warm pitta or toast.

SERVES 4

4 thick slices of sourdough bread, crusts removed

170g smoked cod's roe

1 clove of garlic, peeled and mashed

200g crème fraîche

the juice of ½ lemon

a glug of good olive oil

freshly ground black pepper

Smoked haddock and kale lasagne

SERVES 4

800g smoked haddock fillets

500ml whole milk mixed with 500ml water

1 onion, peeled and cut into wedges

1 bay leaf

a few cloves

a few black peppercorns

50g salted butter

50g plain flour

1 tbsp coarse-grain mustard

1 tbsp fresh chives, chopped

freshly grated nutmeg

2 large free-range egg yolks

sea salt and freshly ground black pepper

150g dried lasagne sheets

200g curly kale, blanched and refreshed

4 tbsp freshly grated Parmesan cheese

This is something a bit different – comfort food at its best. In my opinion, smoked haddock is one of the cheapest luxury ingredients you can buy. It really is delicious, the subtle smoky flavour it gives to dishes putting it on a par with foie gras and caviar. As for kale, it's more robust than spinach, but just as tasty and very good for you.

Place the smoked haddock in a medium-sized pan and cover with the milk and water. Add the onion, bay leaf, cloves and peppercorns and simmer gently for about 5 minutes, until the fish starts to flake. Take the fish out of the pan and remove the skin and any bones, then flake the fish while it is still hot, as this will make it easier. Set the fish aside and strain the poaching liquid into a jug.

In a clean pan melt the butter and stir in the flour, cooking the mixture for about 2–3 minutes. Slowly add the milk back into the pan, stirring all the time, until you have a smooth, velvety mixture like a savoury custard (you may not need to use all the liquid for this). Add the mustard, chives and a good grating of nutmeg, beat in the egg yolks and set aside. Season to taste with salt and pepper. Now you can put the lasagne together.

Preheat the oven to 190°C/gas mark 5. Lightly grease a medium-sized ovenproof dish. Pour a little sauce on the base of the dish and arrange pasta sheets on top. Scatter over some kale and a third of the fish, then pour over a little more sauce. Repeat the layers twice – pasta, kale, fish. Finish with the last of the sauce and sprinkle with the Parmesan. Bake for about 25–30 minutes, until hot and bubbling. Allow to stand for about 10 minutes before serving. This is an all-in-one dish but by all means have a nice dressed green salad to go with it.

Soused herring salad
with soured cream dressing

This is a very quick and tasty dish – simple to prepare, with maximum flavour. Obviously you need to buy top-quality soused herrings (also known as rollmops). They should be nice and firm, with plenty of sliced onions in them. If you want to make this into a true Scandinavian feast, add some boiled new potatoes and sliced beetroot. An iced vodka would go down very well too!

Unroll the herrings and remove the onions, setting them aside. Cut each herring into 3 pieces. Pour the soured cream into a bowl and season well, stir in the lemon zest, juice and chives. Put the lamb's lettuce, herring pieces and onions in a larger bowl and gently stir in the dressing. Lay the buttered bread on a plate, then heap the salad on top of it. Crack some more pepper over everything and serve.

SERVES 4

400g soused herrings or rollmops

150–200ml soured cream

sea salt and freshly ground black pepper

the zest and juice of 1 small lemon

a small handful of fresh chives, chopped

70g lamb's lettuce

4 slices of buttered granary bread

Salted and marinated anchovies on caramelized onions

SERVES 4

400g all-butter puff pastry

plain flour, for dusting

4 tbsp olive oil

2 large onions, peeled and thinly sliced

1 sprig of fresh thyme, leaves only

sea salt and freshly ground black pepper

50g salted anchovies in oil, drained

50g marinated white anchovy fillets in oil, drained

24 small black olives, pitted and halved

In the South of France they make a lovely type of pizza called pissaladière, which is salty and delicious. To add my own twist, I use a good-quality puff pastry instead of the bread dough and mix in marinated anchovies with the salted ones to give it a nice sharp kick. Use small good-quality black olives for this, as it's a simple recipe which relies on the ingredients.

Roll out the puff pastry on a floured surface into a neat square about 5mm thick, then leave it to rest in the fridge for about 20 minutes. Meanwhile preheat the oven to 200°C/gas mark 6. Remove the pastry from the fridge and cut into 4 perfect squares. Place these on a non-stick baking sheet. Lay another baking sheet directly on top of the pastry and bake for about 20 minutes, until the pastry is crisp and golden brown. Once cooked remove the pastry from the tray and leave to cool on a wire rack.

In a large pan heat the oil, add the sliced onions and thyme, and season well. Cook on a high heat so that the onions get nicely roasted and golden brown, then turn them down to finish cooking. They should be soft, sweet and delicious. While they cool slightly, cut the anchovies in half lengthways.

Now you are ready to assemble the dish. Take a piece of pastry and spread a quarter of the onion mix evenly over it. Criss-cross the different anchovies over the onions and season with pepper. Finally dot over the olive halves and serve. These are delicious on their own or with a simple green salad.

Curried mackerel kedgeree

Kedgeree was a popular Victorian breakfast dish, brought to England when the British colonials returned with an abundance of spices and ideas. Traditionally this would be made with smoked haddock, but I've swapped that for the richer, stronger-tasting mackerel. I tend to make my kedgeree more like a curry, rather than just curry-flavoured rice, so this is quite a bit different from the standard recipe. It makes a great fiery breakfast on a cold winter's day or a good supper dish, depending on your mood.

In a large frying pan bring the stock to the boil. Meanwhile, in a second pan melt the butter and oil, add the garlic and onion and let them gently sweat for a couple of minutes. Add the ginger and curry powder and cook for a further 3 minutes, then add the rice, stirring a couple of times to coat it in the oil and butter.

Gradually add the hot stock, making sure you stir well after each addition. Overall this should take about 20 minutes. Carefully flake the mackerel into the rice, checking to make sure there are no bones, and stir. Divide the kedgeree between warmed serving plates, sprinkle on the coriander and chilli, then top with the quartered eggs. Season and serve immediately. For that extra touch, a spoon of mango chutney on top is lovely.

SERVES 4

1 litre white chicken stock (see page 239)

25g salted butter

1 tbsp olive oil

1 clove of garlic, crushed

1 onion, peeled and chopped

a small knob of fresh ginger, peeled and finely chopped

1 tsp curry powder

225g basmati rice, rinsed well

375g peppered smoked mackerel fillet, without the skin

a small bunch of fresh coriander, chopped

1 red chilli, deseeded and finely chopped

4 large free-range eggs, boiled for 6 minutes, cooled, shelled and quartered

sea salt and freshly ground black pepper

Quick paella
with hot-smoked salmon

SERVES 4

1 tbsp olive oil

1 onion, peeled and sliced

1 clove of garlic, peeled and crushed

110g chorizo sausage or home-made salami (see page 234), sliced

1 tsp smoked paprika

300g long-grain rice

900ml–1 litre hot white chicken stock (see page 239)

200g frozen peas

sea salt and freshly ground black pepper

250g hot-smoked salmon fillet, skinned and flaked

1 lemon, cut into wedges

Not the traditional paella, but close and just as delicious. Hot-smoked fish is actually cooked all the way through, so I would just flake the salmon in large chunks over the finished rice and let the heat warm it gently. My home-made salami recipe goes perfectly alongside, as it's very similar to chorizo.

Heat the oil in a deep frying pan and cook the onion and garlic for 5 minutes without browning. Add the chorizo and fry until it releases its oils, then stir in the smoked paprika and rice. Keep stirring until the rice is coated in oil before pouring in the stock. Bring to the boil and simmer for 15 minutes, stirring occasionally. Tip in the peas and cook for about 5 minutes more, until the rice is done. Check for seasoning and serve immediately, finishing with the flakes of salmon and lemon wedges.

Fresh fish

We are all aware that overfishing in certain waters and of certain species has become a massive and potentially disastrous problem. However, there are still good sustainable stocks that can be eaten guilt-free and I know that cod, if sourced wisely, can still be on the menu. Thanks to groups like the Marine Stewardship Council (MSC) and the Sustainable Restaurant Association (SRA), there is hopefully light at the end of the tunnel.

Non-salt cod brandade

Spanish hake soup

Atlantic halibut steaks 'coq au vin'

Pot roast red mullet with chunky vegetables

Sea bream stuffed with sausage meat

Lemon sole fingers with mushy peas and tartare sauce

Poached sea trout with green sauce

Monkfish and red wine stew with sorrel mash

Dover sole 'Véronique'

Spiced mackerel with horseradish potato salad

Non-salt cod brandade

SERVES 4

300g potatoes, peeled and cubed

sea salt and freshly ground black pepper

750ml whole milk

100ml double cream

1 bay leaf

1 sprig of fresh thyme

400g cod fillet or trimmings

50ml extra virgin olive oil

1 clove of garlic, peeled and thinly sliced

2 large free-range egg yolks

a bunch of spring onions, sliced

Traditionally this French classic is made with salt cod, which has to be soaked for hours to remove the excess salt content, but I'm going to use fresh cod for this recipe as it works just as well. Make sure that your garlic is properly toasted, as this gives the brandade a wonderful depth of flavour, adding a whole new dimension. This dish is perfect for using up trimmings, so if you find yourself with tail pieces or offcuts, make sure to save them.

Put the potatoes in a pan, cover with water, add a pinch of salt and bring to the boil. Simmer until tender, then drain and keep them warm.

In a large pan bring the milk, cream, bay leaf and thyme to the boil. Simmer for 5 minutes, then remove from the heat and leave to infuse for 20 minutes. Bring the mixture back to the boil and add the cod. Reduce heat and gently poach for 6–8 minutes, depending on how thick the cod is. Be careful not to boil or overcook the fish. Remove from the heat and allow to cool for about 10 minutes, then drain the cod, reserving the milk.

Preheat the oven to 220°C/gas mark 7. Meanwhile, warm the oil through in a frying pan, add garlic slices and toast until golden. Add the oil and garlic to a food processor, together with the fish, the potato and about 150ml of the strained milk. Purée in a food processor to obtain a soft consistency, adding more milk if necessary.

Transfer the cod mixture to a large bowl, stir in the egg yolks and spring onions and check the seasoning. I like mine fairly peppery. Divide the mixture between four 200ml ovenproof dishes, then bake for 12–15 minutes, until golden and bubbling. Serve with thin slices of baguette fried in olive oil, or just some fresh crusty bread.

Spanish hake soup

SERVES 6

500g skinned hake fillets

3 tbsp olive oil

1 large onion, peeled and chopped

1 large fennel bulb, stalks discarded and bulb chopped

2 red peppers, deseeded and diced

3 large cloves of garlic, peeled and chopped

50g small chorizo piquante, sliced

2 x 400g tins of chopped tomatoes

1 tbsp tomato purée

400ml dry sherry

the juice of 1 large lemon

1 sprig of fresh thyme, leaves only

3 tsp fresh tarragon, chopped

sea salt and freshly ground black pepper

As with many of the recipes in this book, I came up with the idea for this soup when attempting to fight off hunger with the few ingredients I had to hand. I set out to make a fish soup, as I had some lovely fillets of hake, but then realized that I didn't have much else. After a bit of scavenging, I found some sherry and some tinned tomatoes in the cupboard, plus an old red pepper and half a chorizo in the fridge, and thus my Sarge classic was born. A few extras have now been added of course, to slightly improve it.

Cut the fish into large chunks about 5cm wide. Heat the oil in a large pan and add the onion, fennel, red peppers and garlic. Cover the pan and sweat gently until the vegetables are really soft, then add the chorizo.

After 5 minutes stir in the tomatoes and tomato purée and cook for a few minutes. Add the fish and 500ml water, 275ml sherry, the lemon juice, thyme and tarragon. Cover the pan and bring to the boil slowly. Simmer gently for about 10 minutes, keeping the lid on but stirring from time to time, until the fish falls completely apart. Add the rest of the sherry, then season to taste.

Allow the soup to cool before puréeing it in a liquidizer. Taste and adjust the seasoning as required, then pour into four warm soup bowls. If you like you can add a few cubes of firm chorizo or cooked prawns to the soup.

Atlantic halibut steaks 'coq au vin'

As with so many fish, you need to be concerned about where your halibut has come from. Luckily, with the number of regulations in place these days, your fish should be guaranteed sustainable. Farmed halibut is of a very good quality and gets a beautiful colour when roasted. Its firm, meaty texture means it works very well with this robust garnish.

Preheat the oven to 180°C/gas mark 4.

In a non-stick pan heat some olive oil and fry the halibut steaks on both sides until golden brown, then add the thyme and transfer to a baking sheet. Cook the fish in the oven for 4–5 minutes, then remove to a plate and keep warm.

Meanwhile, in a large pan fry the lardons in oil until brown and crisp. Add the onions and mushrooms and colour them. Pour in the red wine and reduce by half, then add the brown chicken stock and simmer for about 5 minutes, until the vegetables are cooked and the sauce has reduced to a light glaze.

Mix the lemon zest and parsley together. Melt a little butter in a pan and quickly sauté the spinach. Season, then drain and place in the middle of the serving plates. Top with the halibut steaks and pour the sauce over and around. Finally sprinkle with the zest and parsley mix.

SERVES 4

olive oil

4 halibut steaks (cut across on the bone), about 200g each

1 sprig of fresh thyme

100g smoked pancetta, cut into lardons

20 baby onions, peeled

20 button mushrooms, cleaned

200ml red wine

500ml brown chicken stock (see page 238)

the zest of 1 lemon

¼ bunch of fresh flat-leaf parsley, leaves only, roughly chopped

25g butter

500g spinach

sea salt and freshly ground black pepper

Pot roast red mullet
with chunky vegetables

If possible, good large mullets are best for this, so buy 4 individual fish. The trick is to cook them whole, with the guts intact. Certain fish are much better with the guts in, and red mullet liver is a particular delicacy. If you have trouble finding red mullet, gurnard is a good alternative and is probably a bit cheaper, although it is considerably bonier. This is a rustic, full-flavour one-pot meal, so don't worry if it looks slightly rough around the edges. Roll up your sleeves, get a crusty loaf and dig in!

Preheat the oven to 180°C/gas mark 4.

In a casserole pan large enough to hold all the ingredients, heat half the olive oil and fry the fish on both sides, then transfer to a plate. Heat the remaining oil in the casserole. Add the onions and fennel and fry for 5 minutes. Sprinkle over the flour, then blend in the wine and stock. Bring up to the boil and stir until the sauce has thickened slightly.

Add the butternut squash and thyme, season and cover with a lid. Simmer for 10 minutes, until the squash is starting to soften. Place the mullets on top of the vegetables, replace the lid and transfer to the oven for about 20–25 minutes, until the fish comes away from the bone easily. Sprinkle over the parsley and check the seasoning. Serve with some good crusty bread to mop up the juices.

SERVES 4

4 tbsp olive oil

4 red mullets (400g each), scaled but guts left in (if you dare)

2 onions, peeled and roughly chopped

2 fennel bulbs, stalks discarded and bulbs cut into 2cm pieces

2 tbsp plain flour

300ml white wine

450ml white chicken stock (see page 239)

1 large butternut squash, peeled and cut into 2cm pieces

3 sprigs of fresh thyme

sea salt and freshly ground black pepper

½ bunch of fresh flat-leaf parsley, leaves only, roughly chopped

Sea bream
stuffed with sausage meat

SERVES 4

4 sea bream (600g each), scaled and gutted

sea salt and freshly ground black pepper

4 good-quality pork sausages

4 sprigs of fresh thyme

16 slices of very smoky streaky bacon

olive oil

I got this idea from an old recipe for cooking freshwater perch. Back in the days when people hadn't even tried sea bass it was normal to eat more freshwater fish and it's a shame that we don't still. Pike and perch were often on the dinner table, mostly stuffed with forcemeat of some kind to make them go further. I have chosen sea bream as it is more user-friendly, but if you fancy going fishing for perch, then by all means use that instead.

Preheat the oven to 200°C/gas mark 6.

Make sure that your fish are nice and clean and dry, especially in the cavity. Season the cavity well, then set the fish aside. Squeeze the sausage meat from the skins and into a bowl. Beat well to make sure that it's mixed together, then divide the meat between the fish, pushing it as deep as you can inside the cavity. The space is quite small, but you can get a surprising amount inside and the bacon will hold everything in.

Once your fish are stuffed, season them well and place a sprig of thyme on each one. Lay 4 slices of bacon out on a work surface and use the back of your knife to slightly stretch them before placing the fish, thyme side down, on top. Wrap the bacon around the fish, then turn the parcel over so that the ends of the bacon are underneath the fish (this helps keep it on during cooking).

Place the fish on a lightly oiled baking sheet, then drizzle a little more oil over the top. Bake for 20–30 minutes, until the bacon is crispy, the sausage meat is cooked and the fish falls away gently from the bone.

Lemon sole fingers
with mushy peas and tartare sauce

SERVES 4

4 lemon sole fillets (100g each), skinned

seasoned plain flour

1 large free-range egg, beaten

60g Japanese breadcrumbs

150g tinned marrowfat peas

50g salted butter

5 sorrel leaves, chopped (8–10 basil leaves could be used as an alternative)

1 tbsp malt vinegar

sea salt and freshly ground black pepper

oil for frying

1 lemon, cut into wedges

for the tartare sauce

50g mayonnaise

30g gherkins, roughly chopped

30g salted capers

1 tbsp fresh flat-leaf parsley, leaves only, roughly chopped

1 tbsp finely chopped shallot

There is something so comforting about fish fingers. Maybe it's that most of us grew up eating them either after or at school. My favourite is a fish finger sandwich, made with soft white bread thickly spread with butter that drips down your chin as you eat. I wouldn't dare ask you to use the fish fingers that we used to eat, but you can make your own and lemon sole is perfect for this. Once filleted, covered in breadcrumbs and fried, they actually look like proper fish fingers and they taste so much better. With some good mushy peas and home-made tartare sauce, they make the perfect light lunch, and you can always double the quantities for a main course.

Place the sole flesh side up on a board and lightly score lengthways through the middle, following the natural line of the fillet. Fold in half lengthways, so you get a double thickness of sole and it looks like a large fish finger. Roll each of these in the flour, the egg and finally the breadcrumbs, then set aside.

Strain off the liquid from the marrowfat peas and heat up with the butter. Mash roughly with the back of a fork, then add the sorrel, a splash of malt vinegar and seasoning.

Mix all the ingredients for the tartare sauce together, taste and season if needed.

Deep-fry the fish fingers in hot oil at 180°C (if you don't have a thermometer, test by sprinkling breadcrumbs, and when they sizzle it's ready) until golden brown and crispy. Drain on kitchen paper and season well. To serve, place a good dollop of mushy peas on each plate and a spoonful of tartare sauce, topping both with a fish finger and a wedge of lemon.

Poached sea trout
with green sauce

This is a light, simple dish that is packed with flavour and ideal for a summer picnic. As always, good-quality fish is a must and it needs to be lightly cooked so it is still a little underdone in the centre. Sea trout has a fairly earthy taste, so the green sauce brings a refreshing tang. This is perfect with a simple green leaf salad or some boiled Jersey royals.

You will need a fish kettle to poach a whole fish, but if you haven't already got one it's a good investment and looks so professional when hung up in your kitchen.

Season your fish inside and out and then gently lay it in the fish kettle. Add the thyme, bay leaves, lemon slices, white wine, white wine vinegar, coriander seeds and peppercorns. Pour in enough water to barely cover the fish and season again. Bring the water to a gentle simmer and place the lid on top of the fish kettle. Leave to simmer for another 2 minutes, then turn off the heat and leave the fish to cool for about 35–40 minutes. By this time it should be cooked to perfection, remaining beautifully moist.

Meanwhile, to make the green sauce place the parsley, coriander, lemon juice, garlic, anchovies, mustard, Tabasco, red wine vinegar and a large pinch of salt in the liquidizer and blitz for a minute or so, just to break it down a bit. Pour in the oil and then blitz again, this time until you have a smooth, bright green sauce. Pour into a sauce boat and set aside.

Remove the fish from the fish kettle and place on a large plate. Gently lift off the skin, then pour the green sauce all over. Let people dive in and help themselves.

SERVES 8

2–2.5kg sea trout, scaled and gutted

sea salt and freshly ground black pepper

1 sprig of fresh thyme

4 bay leaves

1 lemon, sliced into 6

1 glass of white wine

3 tbsp white wine vinegar

10 coriander seeds

10 white peppercorns

for the green sauce

a large bunch of fresh flat-leaf parsley, leaves only

a large bunch of fresh coriander, leaves only

the juice of 1 lemon

2 cloves of garlic, peeled

5 salted anchovies in oil, drained

1 tsp English mustard

a few drops of Tabasco Sauce

2 tbsp red wine vinegar

300ml olive oil

Monkfish and red wine stew
with sorrel mash

SERVES 4

1kg monkfish tail fillet, trimmed of membrane

6 tbsp olive oil

150g smoked streaky bacon, cut into lardons

4 banana shallots, peeled, halved and finely sliced

4 cloves of garlic, peeled and finely sliced

2 bay leaves

1 sprig of fresh thyme

4 tbsp plain flour

300g button mushrooms, cleaned

350g small Chantenay carrots, trimmed and cleaned

500ml dry red wine

500ml brown chicken stock (see page 238)

sea salt and freshly ground black pepper

2 tbsp fresh flat-leaf parsley, leaves only, chopped

500g sorrel (a similar amount of basil leaves could be used as an alternative)

enough warm buttery mashed potato for 4

There are few fish which can stand robust cooking, as they are mostly light in texture and fall apart easily. Monkfish, however, is more like meat and in this instance is perfect for braising in a rich red wine sauce. Sorrel is a fantastic plant with a subtle, vinegary flavour, which makes it not unlike kiwi fruit, and this is perfect to balance the rich, deep flavour of this stew.

First you need to cut your monkfish into good sized chunks, roughly the same size as you would expect stewing steak to be cut. Heat 2 tablespoons of oil in a large, heavy-bottomed, lidded pan over a medium heat and add the lardons, stirring until they get nice and brown. Add the shallots, garlic, bay leaves and thyme, then adjust the heat so that the shallots cook gently for a further 10 minutes, until soft and lightly coloured.

Meanwhile, pat the fish dry with kitchen paper and toss in the flour. Heat 2 tablespoons of oil in a frying pan and briefly brown the fish in batches, so that it cooks quickly and evenly. Rest the fish on kitchen paper to drain as you cook each batch, adding the remaining oil to the frying pan as required.

Now add the mushrooms and carrots to the bacon mixture and fry for 5 minutes. Add the red wine and stock, bring up to the boil and simmer for 5–8 minutes, until the carrots are nearly cooked and the sauce has reduced. Season, then discard the bay leaves and thyme, add the monkfish and sprinkle with the chopped parsley.

Pick the stalks from the sorrel and place them in a colander or sieve, then pour over a kettle of boiling water. Tap the excess water off and dry well with a clean tea towel. Roughly chop the blanched sorrel and add it to the warm, buttery mash. Serve the mash in a big bowl and the monkfish in the pan on the table, allowing everyone to help themselves.

Dover sole 'Véronique'

SERVES 4

4 Dover sole fillets (125g each), skinned

sea salt and freshly ground white pepper

60ml white wine

1 tbsp Noilly Prat

500ml white chicken stock (see page 239)

300ml double cream

2 egg yolks

40 seedless white grapes, peeled

If done correctly, this classic is absolutely delicious. The perfectly cooked fillets of sole are glazed in a vermouth sauce and then would usually be served with peeled Muscat grapes. These can be difficult to find, so you can use normal white seedless grapes, which are nearly as good. This dish requires quite a lot of effort but is definitely worth it.

Place the fillets skinned side up on a board. Using a sharp knife, lightly score each one in half widthways, slicing only halfway through. Fold the fillets in half so you have a double thickness of sole and they look like little parcels. Season the fillets and put them into a tight-fitting shallow saucepan with the wine, Noilly Prat and chicken stock. Cover with a lid and bring to a slow boil before simmering gently for 2–3 minutes.

Remove the fillets carefully to a plate, cover with cling film and keep warm. Reduce the remaining liquid down to about 4–5 tablespoons, then add the cream, keeping back 1 tablespoon, and continue to reduce until the sauce is nice and creamy and coats the back of a spoon a bit like custard. Mix the egg yolks with the remaining cream, so it can be stirred into the sauce easily. Then pour the mixture into the reduced sauce and stir quickly.

Preheat the grill to its highest setting. Taste the sauce and season if necessary. Drain any liquid from the sole fillets and arrange them on a heatproof plate, then spoon over the sauce and glaze under the grill until golden. Garnish with the seedless grapes and serve.

Spiced mackerel
with horseradish potato salad

It's quite amazing how whenever you go sea fishing the one thing you will be sure to catch is a lot of silvery-blue and delicious mackerel. While other fish become more and more expensive to buy, the humble mackerel, so easy to catch and so fantastic to eat, remains very cheap. Hopefully the day will never come when stocks start to dwindle and the price soars. Mackerel is a fish that is packed with flavour and is incredibly good for you, so it's an all-round winner. Some people are put off by the strong 'fishy' taste, but the gentle spicing in the dish helps to balance this out.

Make the horseradish potato salad first. Cook the potatoes in boiling salted water for 10–12 minutes. Drain and cool slightly, then cut in quarters and set aside while you heat some olive oil in a frying pan. When the oil is a medium heat add the potatoes and season, sautéing until they are lovely and golden brown. Drain well on kitchen paper, then put into a mixing bowl. Stir in the shallots, soured cream and horseradish cream, season to taste and mix in the chives. Set aside to serve warm or at room temperature.

Heat the grill to the highest setting. Slash the mackerel three times on each side and place on a baking dish. Mix all the remaining ingredients together in a bowl to form a thick spiced butter and season well with salt and pepper. Rub the butter all over the mackerel, including inside the cavity, then grill for 4–5 minutes on each side until the fish is just firm and cooked through. Serve immediately with the potato salad.

SERVES 4

4 whole medium mackerel, gutted

100g salted butter, softened to room temperature

1 tsp cayenne pepper

2 tsp sweet smoked paprika

1 tsp ground coriander

1 tbsp golden caster sugar

½ tsp English mustard

a few drops of Tabasco Sauce

2 tsp red wine vinegar

for the horseradish potato salad

500g new potatoes

olive oil

sea salt and freshly ground black pepper

2 shallots, peeled and finely chopped

2 tbsp soured cream

2 tbsp horseradish cream

a bunch of fresh chives, finely chopped

Shellfish

I am a great lover of shellfish. To me there is nothing more satisfying than sitting somewhere hot with a bottle of chilled rosé, slurping and sucking your way through a big platter of steamed and raw shellfish. I always find it difficult to understand people who eat fish but claim not to like shellfish. Maybe it's the prehistoric looks of some, or the fact that others are eaten while still alive that is off-putting. For most the king of shellfish is the lobster, but for me it's our humble British crab. The simple recipes included here are not only for hardcore shellfish lovers but also for those yet to be converted.

Mussels in pernod
with garlic frites

Ah, *moules et frites* – a dish with the ability to make you feel you're on holiday wherever you are and whatever mood you're in. For this recipe I have swapped the wine for Pernod, a drink I always have for elevenses when holidaying in France. You need nice large mussels for this. They should be sweet and juicy as well as giving lots of juice to soak up with crusty bread. The fries are tossed in butter, garlic and parsley once crisp – another trick I picked up from Boodle's gentlemen's club.

Melt the butter in a saucepan large enough to hold the mussels. Add the leeks, fennel and garlic and fry gently for about 5 minutes, until the vegetables are softened. Add the mussels to the pan, cover tightly and cook over a medium heat for 4–5 minutes, until the shells open, shaking the pan occasionally. Stir in the Pernod and 125ml water, then bring back to the boil. Discard any unopened mussels. Carefully pour the cooking liquid into a small pan and set the covered pan of mussels aside. Stir the cream into the cooking liquid and heat gently without boiling. Season to taste with sea salt and freshly ground black pepper.

Meanwhile, heat the oil to 140°C and fry the potatoes in the usual fashion until they are soft, then drain and turn the heat up to 180°C. Place a large frying pan on the heat and melt the butter, then add the garlic and fry for a few minutes. Dip the chips back in the oil to crisp up, then drain well before tossing them into the garlic butter. Throw in the chopped parsley and toss well again, so the chips are covered in the lovely buttery mixture. Remove to a suitable dish to serve with the mussels and enjoy.

SERVES 4

25g unsalted butter

2 leeks, trimmed and thinly sliced

1 fennel bulb, trimmed and thinly sliced

1 clove of garlic, peeled and crushed

2kg fresh mussels, cleaned

80ml Pernod

85ml double cream

sea salt and freshly ground black pepper

for the garlic frites

vegetable oil for frying

4 Maris Piper potatoes, peeled and cut into matchsticks

50g salted butter

2 cloves of garlic, peeled and crushed

2 tbsp fresh flat-leaf parsley, leaves only, chopped

King prawn and chorizo in a tomato and garlic sauce

SERVES 1

olive oil

3 chorizo sausages, chopped into 1cm slices

350g raw king prawns, peeled and deveined

a pinch of chilli flakes

4 cloves of garlic, peeled and finely chopped

1 x 400g tin of chopped tomatoes

sea salt and freshly ground black pepper

3 tbsp fresh flat-leaf parsley, leaves only, finely chopped

You can use the home-made salami recipe for this dish if you prefer (see page 234), as the smoked paprika gives all the Mediterranean flavour you need. Take note that this is very garlicky. The tube carriage will empty the day after you have eaten it, so make sure that whoever you live with eats it too. A perfect Valentine's treat!

Heat a touch of oil in a medium frying pan over a moderate heat, then add the chorizo and fry for 2–3 minutes, until slightly crispy on each side. Stir in the prawns, chilli flakes and garlic, and sauté for a further 2 minutes, stirring occasionally to stop the garlic burning, until the prawns are just cooked. Add the tomatoes and leave to simmer for 5–10 minutes, until things have thickened to a sauce-like consistency. Season and add the parsley for a nice earthy flavour.

Brown crab
and ginger gratin
with preserved lemons

SERVES 8

200g brown crab meat

150g crème fraîche

450g white crab meat, picked

the zest of 1 lemon

1 preserved lemon, rinsed,
  flesh removed and skin
  finely diced

1 tsp finely chopped stem
  ginger

2 medium free-range egg yolks

sea salt and freshly ground
  black pepper

25g fresh breadcrumbs

25g Parmesan cheese, finely
  grated

As I have already said, I adore crab, and this is a great recipe, especially for dinner parties, as it is prepared in advance and can be served in the shell. All the flavours work really well together. Preserved lemons are very easy to make and will look great in your kitchen. The recipe is on page 232, but you will need to make them a month or so in advance!

Preheat the grill to hot.

Mix the brown crab meat and crème fraîche in a food processor until smooth. Place the white crab meat in a large bowl, checking for any bits of shell, and add the lemon zest, preserved lemon and ginger, then gently mix in the brown crab mixture. Add the egg yolks, season well and then mix again. If you have the crab shells, wash them well and spoon the mixture directly into them; otherwise, you can use gratin dishes.

Sprinkle the breadcrumbs and Parmesan over the top, then place under a hot grill for a couple of minutes until the surface is golden and bubbling. This would be great served with Melba toast and a frisée salad.

Lobster thermidor

SERVES 4

2 cooked lobsters (each about 700g)

25g salted butter

3 large shallots, peeled and finely chopped

100ml dry white wine

400ml hot white chicken stock (see page 239)

100ml double cream

4 tbsp fresh chives, chopped

a pinch of cayenne pepper

sea salt and freshly ground black pepper

30g Parmesan cheese, finely grated

This dish is from the days when grand hotel dining ruled the country and the chefs who ran their kitchens were the culinary stars. The Daddy of them all was Auguste Escoffier and I often wonder what he would make of today's chefs. I can imagine his dismay with a young chef for overcooking the lobster or making the sauce too strong. It's not often found on menus any longer – I'm not really sure why – but I love it and so will you.

First you need to prepare the lobsters. Remove the claws, then crack them by gently hitting with a rolling pin. Remove the meat in large pieces and place in a bowl, making sure that you take out the thin blade bone. Remove and discard the legs. Cut the lobsters in half lengthways, first through the head, between the eyes, then turn them around and continue to cut through the tail.

Take the tail meat from each lobster half and cut into nice big pieces, adding it to the bowl with the claw meat. Remove the red roe, if any is present, and add this also to the bowl as it has a great flavour. Remove and discard the long, thin black line running the length of the body. Transfer the empty shells to a baking tray.

To make the sauce, melt the butter in a frying pan and cook the shallots for 3–4 minutes, until they begin to soften. Add the white wine and let it bubble for a few minutes to burn off the alcohol, then pour in the hot chicken stock and boil for about 5 minutes, until the sauce has reduced by half. Stir in the cream and cook gently for a further 5 minutes, until the sauce has a good coating consistency. Take off the heat and stir in the chopped chives and cayenne. Season to taste.

Preheat the grill to medium-high. Pour the sauce over the lobster bowl and mix well, checking the seasoning again, then divide the meat evenly between the lobster shells and sprinkle with the Parmesan. Grill for 3–4 minutes, until golden and bubbling. Serve immediately, with a garnish of green salad and fine herbs.

Deep-fried oysters
with fried spices

If you're feeling adventurous and don't mind a bit of preparation, these are the ultimate snack to go with a few beers. They have everything that needs to be quenched with an ice-cold pint: crunch, salt, spice and heat.

Heat vegetable oil in a deep-fat fryer to 180°C. Dredge the oysters in plain flour, dust off any excess, then dip them in the beaten egg, making sure they are completely covered, followed by the breadcrumbs. Place them in the deep-fat fryer for 2–3 minutes, until golden brown. Remove from the oil using a slotted spoon and drain on kitchen paper.

For the fried spices, heat about 5–6 tablespoons of vegetable oil in a non-stick pan until fairly hot. Add the garlic slices, chillies and spring onions and fry gently until they become crisp but not too brown. Drain on kitchen paper and season really well with salt. As the spices cool they will become lovely and crunchy.

To eat, just take a deep-fried oyster and sprinkle liberally with the crisp, dry spices. If you like the taste, a squeeze of lime juice goes very well too.

SERVES 4

vegetable oil

16 oysters, shucked

100g plain flour

100g Japanese breadcrumbs

2 large free-range eggs, beaten

3 cloves of garlic, peeled and sliced

2 large red chillies, sliced and seeds left in

a bunch of spring onions, sliced

sea salt

limes (optional)

Whelk stir-fry
with crispy noodles

SERVES 4

2 tbsp groundnut oil

500g whelks, precooked and thinly sliced

250g bamboo shoots, drained and cut into thin strips

2 cloves of garlic, peeled and sliced

1 tbsp grated fresh ginger

2 tbsp soy sauce

1 tbsp oyster sauce

1 tbsp sesame oil

a bunch of spring onions, sliced

½ bunch of fresh coriander, leaves only, chopped

sea salt and freshly ground black pepper

for the crispy noodles

225g dried fine egg noodles

3 tbsp peanut or groundnut oil

Whelks are not commonly eaten any more, especially in the home, but they are delicious. In Australia people eat a shellfish called abalone, which is extremely rare and costs a fortune, but whelks are almost exactly the same and much cheaper. They lend themselves well to Asian spices and the crispy noodles add a great texture.

Heat the groundnut oil in a wok or large frying pan at high heat until it is just beginning to smoke. Add the whelks and bamboo shoot slices and stir-fry for about 3 minutes, then remove and set aside. Add the garlic and ginger to the wok and stir-fry for about 2 minutes, then add the soy sauce, oyster sauce and sesame oil, together with the whelks and bamboo shoots. Continue to stir-fry for another 3 minutes, or until all the liquid is evaporated and the whelks are nice and glossy. Now add the spring onions and coriander. Season, toss well, then remove from the heat and keep warm.

Blanch the fresh egg noodles for 2–3 minutes in a large pan of boiling salted water, until just tender. Drain well and set aside. Heat a frying pan over a high heat, then add 1½ tablespoons of peanut oil. Spread the drained noodles evenly over the base of the pan, then turn the heat to low and allow them to fry gently for 4–5 minutes, until golden brown and crisp on the bottom.

Gently flip the noodles over, adding another 1½ tablespoons of peanut oil to the pan. Cook for a further 3–4 minutes, until the noodles are golden brown and crisp all over. Remove from the pan and drain on kitchen paper. Place the noodles in the middle of a warm plate and spoon the whelks on top.

Carpet shell clam and mushroom stew

SERVES 4

50g unsalted butter

2 cloves of garlic, peeled and crushed

2kg carpet shell clams, cleaned (you could use palourde clams instead)

60ml white wine

1 sprig of fresh thyme

500g fresh girolles, or mushrooms of your choice, trimmed and cleaned

sea salt and freshly ground black pepper

½ bunch of fresh flat-leaf parsley, leaves only, chopped

the juice of ½ lemon

This is like a ragout really. The flavours of the clams and mushrooms go brilliantly together. Try not to cook the clams too long, as they will become tough and chewy. You can use a variety of mushrooms as the season changes: my favourite for this dish are girolles, but a good old-fashioned flat cap (sliced) works just as well.

In a pan big enough to hold all the clams, melt half the butter and add the garlic. Cook for about 2 minutes to soften and release the flavour of the garlic, then turn up the heat and throw in the clams. Cover with a tight-fitting lid and shake the pan, then cook for a minute or so. Remove the lid and add the wine and thyme before replacing it and cooking for about 5 minutes, until all the clams have opened. Drain the clams, being sure to reserve the liquid. Quickly pick the clams from their shells and set aside to keep warm.

In a frying pan melt the remaining butter and add the girolles. Season them well and cook gently for 2–3 minutes. Add the clams and liquor to the mushroom mix, then boil rapidly to reduce the sauce slightly. When the sauce is nice and glossy add the parsley and lemon juice and stir. Serve the clams in warm bowls, with crusty buttered bread to mop up the juices.

Pan-fried scallops
with chorizo

I must admit that I'm not really a big fan of scallops, as I find they can be very rich and sometimes too sweet. Ironically, I prefer them raw, when the flavour is much lighter and more savoury. I have included this recipe, though, because almost everyone I have ever met absolutely adores scallops and I do enjoy preparing and cooking them. You will find that a lot of chefs match scallops with black pudding, but for this dish I've paired them with chorizo – or you could also use my home-made salami (see page 234) – which gives a nice spicy edge that helps to cut through the richness of the scallops.

Heat the olive oil in a wide, heavy-based frying pan and lightly sauté the chorizo slices until golden brown. Transfer to a warm plate and set aside. Season the scallops and add to the hot pan with a few knobs of butter. Fry for 1–1½ minutes on each side, until golden brown and just cooked. Transfer to a warm plate.

Stir the lime juice, sugar and sesame oil together and pour into the hot pan, scraping the bottom with a wooden spoon to deglaze. Take off the heat and set aside.

Divide the salad between four plates, heaping it in the centre. Arrange the chorizo and scallops around the edge, spoon over the warm dressing and serve.

SERVES 4

2 tbsp olive oil

200g chorizo or home-made salami (see page 234), sliced on the diagonal

12 large scallops

sea salt and freshly ground black pepper

a few knobs of salted butter

the juice of 1 lime

½ tsp caster sugar

a dash of sesame oil

100g mixed salad leaves

Cockles in devil sauce

2kg fresh cockles, soaked in water for several hours

3 tbsp olive oil

2 large cloves of garlic, peeled and finely chopped

1 large red chilli, thinly sliced

1 tbsp dark soy sauce

½ tbsp sherry vinegar

1 tbsp lemon juice

a dash of Lea & Perrins

1 bay leaf

1 heaped tsp sugar

freshly ground black pepper

4 large spring onions, chopped

Cockles are really just little bits of protein that need love and attention to make them into something special and this dish does just that. They are perfect poured over toasted thick-cut sourdough bread, which will soak up all the sauce, and they make a great snack to accompany drinks, as they're spicy and salty.

First scrub the cockles and discard any that are open. Then, using your largest saucepan, heat the olive oil and cook the garlic and chilli for 30 seconds. Now add the soy sauce, vinegar, lemon juice, Lea & Perrins, bay leaf, sugar and a generous amount of black pepper.

When the mixture is simmering, tip in the cockles and give everything a quick stir. Cover and cook over a medium-high heat. After a couple of minutes, give another quick stir, replace the lid and cook until all the cockles are open. Stir in the chopped spring onions and serve immediately on toasted sourdough.

Potted crayfish tails

SERVES 6

200g unsalted butter

1 tsp cayenne pepper

1 tsp ground nutmeg

1 tsp ground mace

5 drops of Tabasco Sauce

450g crayfish tails, peeled and cooked

sea salt and freshly ground black pepper

to serve

watercress leaves

lemon wedges

brown bread or buttered toast

I was going to include potted shrimps in this book, but it seems that there are recipes for those everywhere now, so I kept the idea but changed the main ingredient. The seasonings and method are pretty much exactly the same and the outcome is just as nice, but using beautiful freshwater crayfish tails will give a different texture to the dish and be somewhat cheaper too.

Melt the butter in a pan with the cayenne pepper, nutmeg, mace and Tabasco. Once melted, add the crayfish tails. Stir well over the heat and season. Place the crayfish in ramekins or little dishes and press down. Top with the butter from the bottom of the pan and chill in the fridge. Serve with watercress, lemon wedges and brown bread or hot buttered toast.

Cheap cuts

One day I hope to devote a whole book to cheap cuts, as there is so much you can do with the more economical parts of both meat and fish. Despite trying, and in the process being told off by my publisher, I can't squeeze them all into just one chapter. I have also kept it quite safe, not including things like hearts, sweetbreads, lights (lungs) and fries (balls), and going nowhere near cod's tongues or monkfish liver, but the day will come when I will be allowed and I can't wait. The recipes in this chapter are really worth a try. They're a great way to enjoy some of the more forgotten cuts of meat that our grandparents would have seen as a real treat. (And just between ourselves, I couldn't resist slipping in some brains!)

Shoulder of pork with pears and perry

Boiled salt beef and carrots with dumplings

Low and slow oxtail with bashed neeps

Lamb's kidney pilaf

Mum's savoury mince with boiled potatoes

Pork faggots and marrowfat peas

Jacob's ladder and mash

Brains and brawn

Sweet and sour pork cheeks with noodles

Veal kidneys with creamed onions

Shoulder of pork
with pears and perry

SERVES 6–8

1.5–1.8kg pork shoulder, boned and rolled

sea salt and freshly ground black pepper

4 medium-firm pears, like Comice, peeled and quartered

2 heads of garlic, broken into cloves, skin on

6 bay leaves

4 cinnamon sticks

4 star anise

200ml cider vinegar

570ml perry

a pinch of sugar

I wouldn't necessarily say that pork shoulder is a cheap cut, but it does go a long way, so you get great value for your money. It is better cooked on the bone, but if you can only find one without don't worry. Perry is cider made from pears and it goes very well with this dish, creating some delicious juices at the bottom of the pan. This is a pork lover's dream, with fantastic crackling and meltingly soft, sweet meat. It serves 6-8 people, but I love it cold in a sandwich the next day, so don't worry if you have lots left.

Preheat the oven to 220°C/gas mark 7.

Rub the pork shoulder all over with salt and pepper. Use a lot of seasoning, as it is a large piece of meat. Place the meat in a deep ovenproof dish and roast for 40 minutes, or until the skin has crackled and taken on a nice colour.

Transfer to a plate and drain off any excess fat (keep the fat for your roast potatoes, which will go perfectly). Add the pear quarters, garlic, bay leaves, cinnamon and star anise to the dish, then place the pork back on top. Pour the cider vinegar and perry around the sides of the pork, cover with a lid or tin foil and return to the oven. Turn the oven down to 160°C/gas mark 3 and cook for about 3–4 hours. Once the crackling is crispy and the meat meltingly soft, the pork is done and can be transferred to a plate.

If the crackling is a bit soft, peel it off the meat gently (it should come away easily) and put it back in the oven on a tray at 220°C/gas mark 7 for about 10 minutes, until it is crispy.

In the bottom of the dish you will have an amazing mush of pear, juices, whole garlic cloves and spices. Add a pinch of sugar if it's a bit sharp for your taste. Spoon this out into a bowl and serve it over the pork. This dish, my friends, is absolutely incredible!

Boiled salt beef and carrots
with dumplings

1kg salted silverside or brisket, soaked overnight in cold water

4 medium carrots, trimmed, peeled and halved lengthways

4 shallots, peeled

4 cloves of garlic, peeled and cut in half

3 cloves

3 cardamom pods, crushed

10 black peppercorns

2 blades of mace

1 bay leaf

a few sprigs of fresh thyme

for the dumplings

125g plain flour

1 tsp baking powder

salt

60g suet

1 tbsp fresh flat-leaf parsley, leaves only, chopped

1 tbsp English mustard

There is something wonderful about this dish. It is simple, old-fashioned and really tasty. As with a lot of dishes of this type, the best bit for me is the stock you get after long and gentle simmering. It is meaty and a little salty, with a golden hue from the carrots. When you taste it, you just know it could cure any ailment known to man. The meat is, of course, so deliciously tender you can eat the whole dish with a spoon. Is it any wonder that there's a song written about it?

Put the beef into a large saucepan, cover with water and bring to the boil. Skim off any scum that has formed, then add the rest of the ingredients and simmer gently with a lid on for about 2½–3 hours. Remove the carrots after about 30 minutes of cooking, depending on their size, and the shallots after 1 hour, placing them both to one side.

Meanwhile, make the dumplings. Sieve the flour and baking powder into a bowl and add ½ teaspoon of salt. Mix in the suet, parsley and mustard, then add enough water to form a sticky dough. Flour your hands and roll the dough into twelve little balls.

When the beef is cooked, remove it from the pan and keep warm. Poach the dumplings in the cooking liquid for 15 minutes, then remove them and put to one side. Strain the liquid through a fine-meshed sieve and return it to the pan, then boil it until it has reduced by about half, or until it has a good strong flavour. It probably won't need seasoning as a lot of salt will have come out in the cooking liquor.

To serve, reheat the onions, carrots and dumplings in the reduced cooking liquid. Slice the beef and arrange it in a deep plate or bowl with the carrots, onions and dumplings, and spoon over the liquid. It's great with Savoy cabbage or – my favourites – Brussels sprouts.

Low and slow oxtail
with bashed neeps

Few good things come out of a credit crunch, but the fact that oxtail has made it back on to supermarket shelves is, for me at least, a small consolation. Please try this, as it just feels so good gnawing the soft chunks of meat off the bone and makes for a delicious gravy.

Preheat the oven to 160°C/gas mark 3.

Trim the oxtail pieces of excess fat, then season them and lightly dust with flour. In a large, heavy-based pan heat a good glug of vegetable oil and fry the oxtail in batches, changing the oil every time. You need a really good dark colour on the meat, so take your time and do this properly.

Meanwhile, heat the butter in a large ovenproof saucepan and gently cook the onion, garlic and thyme for 3–4 minutes, until the onion is soft and a nice golden-brown colour. Add the rest of the flour and tomato purée and stir well for a few minutes to cook the flour. Gradually add the red wine and stock, stirring well to stop lumps forming, and bring to the boil. Add the pieces of oxtail along with the bay leaves and return to a gentle simmer, then put on a tight-fitting lid and place in the oven.

Check after 2 hours to see if the meat is tender – if it's not falling off the bone, put it back in the oven until it is. You might need to add a little water every now and then if the sauce gets too thick during cooking. This can take 3–4 hours, but the wait will be well worth it. Once the meat is cooked, skim the fat from the sauce with a ladle and then set the oxtail aside to keep warm and steep in the rich gravy.

For the bashed neeps, cover the swede with salted water and bring to the boil. Simmer gently for 10–15 minutes, until the swede is soft, then drain and mash coarsely. Add the butter and season well with black pepper and grated nutmeg to taste. I like a lot of this, as it goes really well with the oxtail. Spoon the oxtail and gravy into warm bowls and add a good dollop of neeps. It's a perfect winter warmer.

SERVES 4

1.5kg oxtail, cut into thick pieces

sea salt and freshly ground black pepper

50g plain flour, plus a little extra for dusting

vegetable oil for frying

60g salted butter

1 onion, peeled and finely chopped

2 cloves of garlic, peeled and crushed

1 sprig of fresh thyme

2 tsp tomato purée

100ml red wine

2 litres brown chicken stock (see page 238)

2 bay leaves

for the bashed neeps

500g swede, peeled and roughly diced

50g salted butter

freshly grated nutmeg

Lamb's kidney pilaf

SERVES 4

6 lamb's kidneys

50g salted butter

4 slices of smoked streaky
bacon, chopped

1 onion, peeled and finely
chopped

250g button mushrooms,
cleaned and sliced

sea salt and freshly ground
black pepper

250g basmati rice, soaked in
cold water for 30 minutes

1 sprig of fresh thyme

the peel and juice of 1 lemon

375ml hot white chicken stock
(see page 239)

½ bunch of fresh flat-leaf
parsley, leaves only, chopped

This is a dish that my girlfriend's mum, Julie, cooks
and I must say that I had never come across it
before I met her. The kidneys impart a great flavour
to the rice as it cooks in the oven and it's a one-pot
dish that is also very good for you. If you are feeling
extravagant you can use veal kidneys for this too,
but Julie merely laughed when I suggested this and
told me that it should really be pig's kidneys, so I'd
best not mess around with her recipe!

Preheat the oven to 180°C/gas mark 4.

Core the kidneys and cut them into small pieces. Heat the
butter in an ovenproof frying pan, add the bacon and onion and
fry until the onion is soft and golden brown. Stir in the kidneys
and seal lightly until they change colour. Add the mushrooms
and fry for 2 minutes, then season and stir in the drained rice.
Cook the rice for about 1 minute to coat the grains, then throw
in the thyme and lemon peel and add the chicken stock.

Bring to the boil, then remove from the heat, put a piece of
parchment paper over the rice (or a lid) and transfer to the
oven. Cook for 15–20 minutes, then remove from the oven and
leave to stand for a couple of minutes. Stir it through gently
with a fork while adding the lemon juice and chopped parsley.
Check the seasoning and serve.

Mum's savoury mince
with boiled potatoes

A simple dish that I had on many a school night. It is basically a lazy shepherd's pie, as the mince is pretty much made in the same way, but the peas are mixed in with it and you serve boiled potatoes on the side instead. The first thing I used to do was to mash all my potatoes up and mix them in with the gravy, then douse the whole lot in loads of Lea & Perrins, much to my mum's disgust and my delight.

Preheat the oven to 180°C/gas mark 4.

Heat an ovenproof casserole and add a little oil. Brown the mince well, then add the onion and garlic and fry gently. When the onions are nice and brown, stir in the carrots, tomatoes and stock. Bring to the boil, season well and add the herbs. Stir, then put in the oven uncovered for 45 minutes.

Remove from the oven and stir in the peas, leaving them for 3 minutes to heat through. Check the seasoning, then add some Lea & Perrins to taste. Serve with lovely big boiled potatoes. I like to use Desiree, as they are waxy and mash up well on your plate. Nice one, Mum!

SERVES 4

vegetable oil for frying

450g good-quality beef or lamb mince

1 large onion, peeled and chopped

1 clove of garlic, peeled and crushed

2 large carrots, peeled and grated

1 x 400g tin of chopped plum tomatoes

570ml white chicken stock (see page 239), with a beef stock cube booster

sea salt and freshly ground black pepper

2 bay leaves

1 sprig of fresh thyme

1 large cup of frozen peas

a good dash of Lea & Perrins

Pork faggots and marrowfat peas

SERVES 4–6

vegetable oil for frying and glazing

1 large onion, peeled and finely chopped

1 clove of garlic, peeled and crushed

1 tsp dried thyme

1 tsp dried sage

500g pork liver, coarsely minced (ask the butcher to do this)

300g pork belly, coarsely minced (again, keep your butcher busy)

70g fresh white breadcrumbs

½ tsp ground mace

sea salt and freshly ground black pepper

2 x 400g tins of marrowfat peas

for the gravy

1 large onion, peeled and finely chopped

30g salted butter

30g plain flour

1 tsp tomato purée

50ml white wine vinegar

a good dash of Lea & Perrins

600ml brown chicken stock (see page 238), with a beef stock cube booster

sea salt and freshly ground black pepper

Now this dish really is my kind of cooking: unpretentious, classic and full of flavour. There's a great butcher called Mike, who owns Drings in Greenwich, and his faggots are delicious. When I am pushed for time to make my own I will pop round and buy a couple of his, which are probably better than mine anyway. Therefore I'm giving you his recipe, but it's how I cook them that makes them great! You will notice that dried herbs are used – this is because I feel they give a better flavour after the slow cooking.

Preheat the oven to 200°C/gas mark 6.

Heat some vegetable oil in a saucepan and fry the onion, garlic, thyme and sage for 3–4 minutes, until the onion is soft but has not coloured. In a large bowl combine the pork liver, pork belly and the breadcrumbs with the onion mix and season well. Leave to sit for about 20 minutes in a cool place to let the flavour start developing and also to firm up slightly, then mould into eight equal-sized balls. Put the faggots in a roasting tray, glaze over with a little vegetable oil and roast for 25 minutes.

While the faggots are roasting you can make the gravy. Fry the onion in the butter on a medium heat until lightly coloured, then add the flour and cook on a low heat for 2–3 minutes. Add the tomato purée, vinegar and Lea & Perrins, then gradually pour in the stock. Bring to the boil, season and simmer for 10 minutes.

Remove the faggots from the oven, drain off the excess oil and pour the gravy over them. Cover with foil, turn the oven down to 160°C/gas mark 3 and cook for 1½ hours. Remove the faggots from the tray carefully with a slotted spoon and place them on a plate. Drain the marrowfat peas and add them to the gravy before placing the faggots back on top. Cook for a further 15 minutes. Add a little more stock or water if the gravy is a bit thick. To serve, place a faggot in a warm bowl and spoon the peas and gravy over the top. Mmmmmmmmmm!

Jacob's ladder and mash

SERVES 4

sea salt and freshly ground
   black pepper

1.5kg beef short ribs, trimmed

1 tbsp plain flour, plus extra
   for dusting

vegetable oil for roasting

1 large onion, peeled and
   roughly chopped

2 large carrots, peeled and
   roughly chopped

6 cloves of garlic, peeled and
   roughly chopped

2 tbsp tomato purée

1 litre beef stock

1.5 litres dark beer (Innis &
   Gunn is wonderful)

100ml dark soy sauce

4 star anise

Short ribs, used everywhere in America, are
starting to catch on in the UK thanks to people like
Fergus Henderson and Mark Hix, who have long
championed this wonderful cut of meat. Basically,
they are ribs taken from the rib of beef, almost like
massive pork spare ribs. However, they are anything
but spare, with lots of beautiful marbled meat
between the large bones. After hours of slow and
careful cooking they will be virtually melting and a
total joy to eat. They also make an amazing sauce,
which simply needs a good buttery mash to soak it
all up.

Preheat the oven to 220°C/gas mark 7.

Season and lightly dust the ribs with flour before roasting in
the oven in a little vegetable oil for 25–30 minutes, until nicely
coloured. Reduce the oven to 160°C/gas mark 3.

Meanwhile, in a heavy-based saucepan, fry the onion, carrots
and garlic until nicely browned, then add the tablespoon of
flour and tomato purée. Cook this for about 5 minutes, then
gradually add the beef stock, beer and soy sauce. Bring to the
boil and add the beef ribs and star anise. Cover and simmer
gently in the oven for 2–2½ hours, until the meat is soft and
tender.

Take the ribs out of the saucepan and remove any fat with
a ladle. Simmer the sauce until it has reduced to about half,
giving it an occasional skim. You want a good consistency for
coating the ribs. Strain into a clean pan through a fine sieve and
return the ribs to the sauce. Simmer them for about 10 minutes
to warm through and become well-coated. Serve with lots of
buttery mash, greens and a large spoonful of horseradish sauce.

Brains and brawn

In the past, when thrift dictated that people make use of every part of the animal, things like brains and brawn, as well as faggots, were eaten regularly. Over the years, the old idea of wasting nothing has gone out of fashion. This is a great shame, because brawn is so good to eat, as long as it is correctly seasoned and nicely spiced. Personally, I prefer to keep the brains separate, serving them fried on a slice of brawn for a nice creamy texture, but you will find there's way more brawn here than brains (nothing like me!), so just incorporate the brains into the mix.

Ask your butcher to remove the ears and tongue from the pig's head, then cut the head into 4 pieces. Keep the ears and tongue.

To make the brine, put the water and salt into a large pan and simmer until the salt has dissolved. Set aside until completely cold, then add the pieces of pig's head, cover and soak for 24 hours. The following day, drain and transfer them to a large stock pot. Cover with cold water, then add the ears, tongue and trotters. Now add the carrots, fennel, thyme, bay leaves, cloves and allspice. Season and bring the mixture slowly to the boil. Skim off any scum that floats to the surface. Once the mixture is simmering, partially cover and keep simmering for about 4 hours, topping up with water as needed. Continue cooking until the meat begins to fall off the bone. Turn off the heat and allow the meat mixture to cool a little.

Remove the head, tongue and trotters from the pan and leave to cool before taking off the skin. Strip off and roughly chop any meat and brain. For the tongue, remove the coarse outer layer of skin, then chop and add to the mix. Also chop the ears and add to the meat mixture. Combine the shallots with the meat and stir in the lemon zest, juice and parsley, then set aside.

Strain the stock and discard the vegetables, herbs and spices. Transfer the meat to a terrine dish or 450g loaf tin that's been lined with cling film, then ladle just enough of the stock over the top to moisten the mixture (2–3 ladlefuls), cover with cling film and place a weight on the top before transferring to the fridge to chill overnight and set. Serve sliced.

SERVES 4

for the brine
3 litres water
1kg salt

for the brawn
1 pig's head
4 pig's trotters
2 large carrots, peeled and roughly chopped
½ fennel bulb, roughly chopped
1 large sprig of fresh thyme
4 bay leaves
3 cloves
6 allspice berries
6 banana shallots, peeled and finely chopped
the zest and juice of 1 lemon
a bunch of fresh flat-leaf parsley, leaves only, roughly chopped
sea salt and freshly ground black pepper

Sweet and sour pork cheeks
with noodles

SERVES 4

2–3 tbsp olive oil

sea salt and freshly ground black pepper

12–16 pig's cheeks (about 700g), trimmed of fat and sinew

3 tbsp honey

2 carrots, peeled and chopped

1 leek, chopped

2–3 sticks of celery, chopped

1 onion, peeled and chopped

2 cloves of garlic, peeled and chopped

1 bay leaf

2 sprigs of fresh thyme

6–8 cloves

1 tbsp tomato purée

750ml brown chicken stock (see page 238)

125ml white wine

Pork cheeks are moist and tender when cooked and have bags of flavour. Because of their size, you will need three or four each, so if you are doing this recipe for six or more make sure you leave plenty of time for preparation, as they can be a bit fiddly. The trick to this dish is to make sure that you caramelize the cheeks well in the honey to get a gorgeous golden-brown colour, otherwise they will look a little anaemic.

Preheat the oven to 160°C/gas mark 3.

Heat the oil in a casserole. Season the cheeks, coat them with 2 tablespoons of honey and brown them over a high heat until golden. Set aside. Heat the remaining oil in a casserole with a tight-fitting lid. Add the carrots, leek, celery, onion and garlic, then cook for 2–3 minutes. Add the bay leaf, thyme, cloves and tomato purée, then cook for a further 2–3 minutes.

Now add the remaining tablespoon of honey and cook for another 2–3 minutes to caramelize all the vegetables. Add the stock and wine and bring to the boil. Season, cover and transfer to the oven. After 2½–3 hours, remove the cheeks from the oven, lift them from the stock and reserve. Strain the stock and place in a medium-sized saucepan. Bring to the boil and allow the mixture to reduce to a semi-sticky sauce before putting the cheeks back into it. Warm through for 2–3 minutes and serve on top of hot buttered noodles.

Veal kidneys
with creamed onions

I adore veal kidneys, having first tasted them in a restaurant in Paris called Brasserie Lipp. As you are probably aware, the fat surrounding the kidney is used for suet. The clever chef there decided to cook the kidney whole, still in its fat! I think he must have lightly salted it first and then studded the fat with rosemary and thyme, before cooking it nice and slowly. As the suet melted, basting the kidney, this imparted an incredible flavour and left it so tender that it was one of the best things I have ever eaten. I have simplified the method and halved the kidneys, but the creamed onions are pretty much the same, as far as I can tell. In fact, mine are probably a bit nicer!

Preheat the oven to 200°C/gas mark 6.

Slice each kidney in half horizontally through the middle so you have 4 pieces. Using a sharp knife and scissors, remove as much of the fat and core as possible, but leave enough intact so the kidney halves don't fall apart. Heat the olive oil in an ovenproof pan on the stove. Season the kidneys and add to the pan, along with the thyme and rosemary. Cook until lightly browned on all sides. Add the knob of butter, then transfer to the oven to cook for 8–10 minutes. Remove the kidneys and keep them warm while they rest for 3 minutes.

To make the creamed onions, start by melting the butter in a large pan. Add the onions, season and cook gently for at least 30 minutes, until they are really soft. Stir occasionally to make sure they don't catch or colour. Add the cider vinegar and juniper berries and continue to simmer until all the liquid has evaporated. Now add the wine and reduce by half, then pour in the cream and stir in the sage leaves. Bring the mixture back to a simmer and leave to cook for about 20 minutes, stirring every now and then. When the onions are thick and velvety put them in a warm bowl and place the kidney halves on top, pouring any resting juices over as well.

SERVES 4

- 2 veal kidneys (each about 400g), trimmed of fat and sinew
- olive oil for frying
- sea salt and freshly ground white pepper
- 1 sprig of fresh thyme
- 1 sprig of fresh rosemary
- a large knob of salted butter

for the creamed onions

- 75g salted butter
- 3 large onions, peeled and thinly sliced
- 50ml cider vinegar
- 4 juniper berries
- 100ml white wine
- 300ml double cream
- 6 fresh sage leaves, shredded

Posh cuts

I suppose this should be called 'Prime Cuts' rather than 'Posh Cuts', but all the recipes in this chapter are for dishes that I would consider a treat rather than ones you might eat at any time. They are more for special occasions or family get-togethers – the sort of thing that has a real wow factor when brought to the table. They are also not the dishes you would want to ruin by overcooking, so please concentrate on these ones! (Yes, Chef!)

Lamb Wellington

SERVES 4
(MAKES 2 WELLINGTONS)

2 lamb cannons, trimmed
    of excess fat and sinew

sea salt and freshly ground
    black pepper

2 tbsp olive oil

2 tsp English mustard

250g chestnut mushrooms,
    cleaned

50g salted butter

1 large sprig of fresh thyme

8 slices of Parma ham

500g all-butter puff pastry

plain flour for dusting

2 large free-range egg yolks,
    beaten with 1 tsp water

This is a very posh dish and requires a certain amount of skill. Having said that, it will impress anyone you invite round for dinner.

Season the lamb cannons well, then in a large pan sear them quickly all over in hot olive oil. While the lamb is still hot, brush with English mustard, then set aside to cool. Meanwhile, chop the mushrooms in a food processor – make sure you pulse-chop them so they retain a texture rather than turning into mush. Heat the olive oil and the butter in the same pan you used for the lamb and fry the mushrooms on a medium heat with the thyme sprig for about 10 minutes, until you have a softened mixture with no moisture left. Season to taste, then remove the mushroom mixture from the pan to cool and discard the thyme.

Overlap two pieces of cling film on a large chopping board. Lay half the Parma ham on the cling film, slightly overlapping, in a double row. Spread half the mushrooms over the ham, then sit a lamb cannon on it. Use the cling film's edges to draw the Parma ham around the lamb, then roll it into a sausage shape, twisting the ends of cling film to tighten it as you go. Repeat this process for the second lamb cannon. Chill the lamb in the fridge while you roll out the pastry.

Roll out half the pastry to the thickness of a pound coin, making sure that it is large enough to wrap around the lamb completely. Unravel the lamb from the cling film and sit it in the centre of the pastry. Egg wash one side of the pastry, then fold the pastry around the lamb and secure it on the egg-washed side. Pinch the ends of the pastry shut and trim off any excess. You should now have a neat cylinder of pastry with no openings. Glaze all over with more egg yolk and, using the back of a knife, mark the lamb Wellington with long diagonal lines, taking care not to cut into the pastry. Repeat with the second Wellington. Chill for at least 30 minutes so the pastry is nice and firm. Meanwhile, preheat the oven to 200°C/gas mark 6.

Place both the Wellingtons on a non-stick tray and bake in the oven until the pastry is golden brown and crisp. This should take around 20–25 minutes, by which time the lamb will be cooked. Remove from the oven and leave to rest for 10 minutes, then trim off the ends and slice in half.

A great roast chicken

SERVES 4

1.8–2kg free-range organic chicken

sea salt and freshly ground black pepper

1 whole bulb of garlic, broken into cloves, unpeeled

1 small lemon

1 small onion, peeled and cut into quarters

a bunch of fresh sage, leaves only

6 rashers of smoked streaky bacon

a bunch of fresh rosemary sprigs

a bunch of fresh thyme

olive oil

Once upon a time, a chicken was a great luxury, more expensive to buy than beef, so it was a real treat to have roast chicken on a Sunday. What's more, the flavour and texture were a million miles away from what they are today. As the population grew, chicken began to be reared intensively, becoming just a protein that doesn't taste of anything – which explains why, whenever people try something unfamiliar, such as frog's legs, they liken it to chicken. So, if it's at all within your budget, please choose a really good-quality chicken and learn to think of roast chicken as a treat again. You might spend more, but I promise you it will be worth it.

Preheat the oven to 220°C/gas mark 7.

Rub the chicken inside and out with lots of salt and pepper. Push the garlic cloves, the whole lemon, onion and the sage into the cavity, then put the chicken in a roasting tray on top of the bacon, rosemary and thyme sprigs and give it a good covering of olive oil. Roast for around 20 minutes. Once the chicken has a nice golden colour all over, turn the oven down to 180°C/gas mark 4 and cook for a further 1 hour 10 minutes, or until the chicken is cooked through (count on 20 minutes per 450g, plus an extra 20 minutes). The chicken is cooked if the juices run clear when it is pierced in the thigh with a skewer.

Remove the chicken from the oven and place on a plate, cover loosely with tin foil and let it rest for at least 20 minutes. This is the most important step, as it is when all the juices get absorbed into the flesh and the meat becomes lovely and tender. Doing the chicken this way DOES NOT give you a crispy skin, but you get the most amazingly moist and tender chicken.

Now remove the lemon and onion from the cavity and discard but keep the lovely soft, plump cloves of garlic. Carve the chicken as you prefer and serve with the garlic, crispy bacon and any juices from the pan. This is delicious to have as a traditional roast dinner or cold in the summer with mayonnaise: either way the chicken is a star again.

Brogdale duck

Brogdale Farm near Faversham in Kent, home to the National Fruit Collection, is a wondrous place. Part of an international programme to protect plant genetic resources for the future, it has over 3,500 named apple, pear, plum, cherry, vine, bush fruit and cob nut cultivars. Brogdale is just round the corner from Read's Restaurant, where I worked for three years, and I often paid them a visit to watch the seasons change – in blossom time the trees are really breathtaking. Which leads to this recipe: it's very hard not to be inspired in a place like that and last time I was there I took a selection of apples home. They quickly turned into a fantastic stuffing for a roast duck, while the leftovers became a delicious apple sauce – the perfect accompaniment to serve with rich and fatty duck.

SERVES 4

25g salted butter

1 medium onion, peeled and finely chopped

10 fresh sage leaves, shredded

110g fresh white breadcrumbs

1 small eating apple (such as Cox's), peeled, cored and coarsely grated

1 medium free-range egg, beaten

1.5kg duck

sea salt and freshly ground black pepper

450g Bramley apples, peeled, cored and sliced

5 cloves

2 tbsp caster sugar

Preheat the oven to 180°C/gas mark 4.

To make the stuffing, melt half the butter in a medium saucepan and cook the onion until softened. Add the sage, then stir in the breadcrumbs, grated eating apple and beaten egg. Prick the skin of the duck all over with a sharp skewer or fork and season the duck well, both inside and out. Push the stuffing into the back cavity, then use the flap of fat at the back of the duck to secure it in place. Put the duck on a wire rack in a roasting tray and roast for roughly 30–35 minutes per 500g, so this recipe should take about 1½ hours. If the juices run clear when the legs are pierced with a skewer, remove from the oven and leave to rest in a warm place. You will be left with loads of beautiful fat, which – as you already know – is perfect for roast potatoes.

To make the apple sauce, place the sliced cooking apples in a saucepan with the cloves, sugar and a little water, just enough to get it started. Cover and cook for 10 minutes, or until the apples are tender, shaking the pan occasionally. Stir in the remaining butter and beat until you have a smooth purée, then pass it through a fine sieve to remove the cloves. To serve, carve the duck as you prefer, then spoon out the stuffing from the cavity and eat with the warm apple sauce.

Pot roast rump of beef

Rump of beef is a delicious cut that we are mostly used to having as steaks, but if you can get a nice whole piece from your butcher, then please try this recipe. Without wishing to cause too much controversy, I personally think that fillet of beef should be banned! Well, maybe not completely, as a good beef Wellington is totally delicious, but it is such a boring cut of meat because there is no fat. Of course, if you buy a good-quality piece of fillet you will have nice marbling running through it, but it's not the same as a lovely creamy slick of fat that crisps up and tastes delicious. You can use sirloin for this recipe, but rump will give you the best flavour and texture.

Preheat the oven to 140°C/gas mark 1.

In a casserole dish melt half of the butter over a high heat, then brown the beef well on all sides. Remove the meat and wipe the dish carefully with some kitchen paper before returning the meat to it. Add the wine, vinegar, thyme, bay leaves and garlic, then season well. Bring it all up to simmering point. Cover the casserole with a tight-fitting lid and transfer to the oven. Cook without lifting the lid for 3 hours, then remove the meat, cover it with foil and leave it to rest for 10 minutes.

Place the casserole dish on the stove and boil to reduce the liquid slightly. Mix the flour and remaining butter to a smooth paste and add this in small pieces, whisking until you have a smooth, slightly thickened sauce. Pour any resting juices into the sauce, then strain it into another saucepan. Add the tarragon and sugar, adjust the seasoning, then carve the meat into thick slices. Lay the meat in a deep serving dish, strain the sauce over and serve.

SERVES 4

30g salted butter

1.5kg rump of beef, rolled

450ml red wine

2 tbsp red wine vinegar

a bunch of fresh thyme

2 bay leaves

1 head of garlic, cut in half, cloves left unpeeled

sea salt and freshly ground black pepper

1 tbsp plain flour

a bunch of fresh tarragon, leaves only

a pinch of sugar

Lemon and sage stuffed loin of pork

SERVES 4–6

2kg boned loin of free-range pork

the zest of 2 lemons

a bunch of fresh sage, leaves only

½ bunch of fresh flat-leaf parsley, leaves only

2 cloves of garlic, peeled and sliced

sea salt and freshly ground black pepper

olive oil

a splash of malt vinegar

I love pig! It is the most versatile animal on the planet and it's just so tasty – I could eat it all day long. This is a posher cut of pork than I would normally use, as I tend to favour the fattier belly and shoulder, but when stuffed like this and cooked slightly pink in the centre it is very tasty. Then, of course, you have the best bit of all, which is the glorious crispy skin, bubbling, crackling and amazing. Just thinking about it as I write makes me salivate and I can almost taste it.

Preheat the oven to its highest setting – about 240°C/gas mark 9.

With a sharp knife, score the skin of the pork loin in a criss-cross pattern. Turn it round so the flesh side is facing upwards and cut a slit along the side of the loin, without going all the way through, to open it out like a butterfly. Cover the flesh with the lemon zest, sage and parsley leaves, then scatter over the garlic. Season generously and drizzle over a little olive oil. Fold back the loin so it looks like the original piece and secure tightly with kitchen string at 3–4cm intervals.

Rub the scored skin with the malt vinegar, which will help to crackle it up, then with a large pinch of salt and a drizzle of olive oil. Place the pork on a baking tray and roast for 15–20 minutes, until the skin is golden and starting to crackle. Turn the oven down to 180°C/gas mark 4 and roast for about 1 hour, until the pork is cooked and tender and very slightly pink in the middle. Rest the pork in a warm place for 10–15 minutes before carving.

New season saddle of lamb

with spring stuffing

SERVES 4

1.3kg boned saddle of lamb

sea salt and freshly ground black pepper

3 tbsp olive oil, plus extra to drizzle

50g wild garlic leaves (or 4 cloves of garlic)

a small handful of fresh flat-leaf parsley, leaves only, chopped

4–6 young carrots, scrubbed and halved lengthways

250g baby courgettes, ends trimmed and halved lengthways

a bunch of large spring onions, trimmed and chopped into large chunks

1 small head of garlic, broken into cloves and unpeeled

2 sprigs of fresh thyme, leaves only, chopped

2 sprigs of fresh rosemary, leaves only, chopped

100ml white wine (or water if you don't have wine to hand)

500ml brown chicken stock (see page 238)

the juice of ½ lemon

Please try to get wild garlic for this recipe as it makes a real difference. I used to holiday a lot in Suffolk and Norfolk and on sunny spring walks through the local woods I would stumble upon carpets of the stuff. If the sun is out you will probably smell it before you see it.

Open out the saddle on a chopping board and rub all over with a pinch each of salt and pepper and a drizzle of olive oil. Chop the wild garlic and parsley and place in a bowl. Add a little seasoning and 3 tablespoons of olive oil and mix into a wet paste. Spread this over the middle of the lamb and under any folds. Fold the sides of the lamb over the stuffing to form a neat log and tie with kitchen string at 6–8cm intervals to hold it together. Rub a little olive oil over the skin and season again generously. Leave it to chill in the fridge for at least an hour to firm up so it holds its shape.

Preheat the oven to 220°C/gas mark 7.

Scatter the vegetables, garlic, thyme and rosemary in a deep roasting tray. Place the saddle of lamb on a rack over the vegetables so that the lamb can flavour them, and pour the wine or water over the vegetables. Roast for 20 minutes, then turn the oven down to 180°C/gas mark 4 and cook for another 20–30 minutes, until the lamb is medium-rare. Remove the lamb and vegetables to a board, cover with foil and rest for 15 minutes.

To make the gravy, spoon off the excess oil in the roasting tin, then put the tin on the stove over a high heat. Pour in the stock, scraping the base of the tin to dislodge any bits. Boil until the liquid has reduced by half and thickened slightly. Taste and adjust the seasoning, then add the lemon juice. Strain the gravy through a sieve into a warm jug. Carve the lamb into thick slices and serve with the roast vegetables and gravy. This is spring on a plate!

Tafelspitz
with apple and horseradish

I had never heard of this before I read Joseph Wechsberg's book *Blue Trout and Black Truffles*, in which he talks about Vienna and the grand restaurants that serve over twenty-four varieties of boiled beef, of which Tafelspitz is one. As far as I can make out, Tafelspitz uses the point end of a rump of beef which is very well aged but, unlike the British version of boiled beef, not salted. It is cooked with the fat on to give moisture and tenderness to the meat and great flavour to the broth. This broth was in fact so good that Viennese diners would often start their meal with a small cupful to get their appetites going.

Place the meat and bones in a very large saucepan and cover with cold water. Bring the water to the boil quite slowly and skim it constantly to remove any fat and scum, as this will result in the finished broth being ultra clear. Fry the onions, cut surface down, in vegetable oil until well browned, then add to the meat with the peppercorns and lovage or parsley, which you've tied with kitchen string so it will be easy to remove later. Bring to the boil gently, again skimming off any scum that rises to the surface. Simmer for 3 hours, then add the carrots, celery and leeks, as well as some more water so that the meat is covered. Bring to the boil again and simmer for another hour. When the meat is meltingly tender, remove it from the stock and keep it warm. Discard the bones and excess fat, the onions and the lovage or parsley. Season and pass the stock through a fine sieve.

Now for the apple and horseradish. Stew the apples until soft, then purée them in a liquidizer. Add the horseradish and season to taste with salt and lemon juice. To serve, cut the meat into thick slices across the grain, then arrange in warmed bowls and pour over a little of the stock. Sprinkle with sea salt and chives. Serve with the vegetables on the side (you may want to pick the peppercorns out before serving). Finally, spoon on a dollop of apple and horseradish and enjoy.

SERVES 6

2–2.5kg rump of beef, with firm white fat (ask your butcher for the point end)

1kg beef bones (with marrow)

2 large onions, peeled and halved

2 tbsp vegetable oil

15 black peppercorns

a bunch of lovage or fresh flat-leaf parsley, leaves only

3 carrots, peeled and roughly chopped

2 large sticks of celery, roughly chopped

2 leeks, roughly chopped

sea salt and freshly ground pepper

a bunch of fresh chives, finely chopped

for the apple and horseradish

2 eating apples (such as Cox's), peeled, cored and quartered

2 heaped tbsp freshly grated horseradish (if fresh is unavailable, horseradish from a jar is an acceptable substitute)

sea salt

lemon juice

Italian rib of veal

SERVES 4

500g rib of veal (also known as veal chop)

6 tbsp olive oil

sea salt and freshly ground black pepper

2 cloves of garlic, peeled and thinly sliced

3 salted anchovies in oil, drained

250g baby spinach

250g tagliatelle

200g tenderstem broccoli

the zest and juice of 1 lemon

30g Parmesan cheese, freshly grated

I don't want to be a crusader, but if you drink milk then you really should eat British rose veal. Yes, it's true that in the past veal wasn't reared in the best of conditions, but all that has changed now. Most people don't realize that in the British dairy industry there is a big problem: male or bobby calves! Of course male calves don't produce milk, so what do you do with them? What usually happens is that they are exported to France or Holland to be reared as veal. Not only does this cause a huge amount of stress to the animals, but conditions abroad are not as good as they are over here. Therefore the more British veal we eat, the less stress bobby calves have to endure. Besides all of this, it is truly delicious, with a firmer, meatier texture than its foreign counterpart, though still meltingly tender.

Preheat the oven to 200°C/gas mark 6.

Rub the meat with a little olive oil, season well all over and sear in a hot non-stick ovenproof pan. Transfer to the oven and roast for 20 minutes. Remove and let it rest in a warm place. Meanwhile, warm 5 tablespoons of olive oil in a large pan and gently fry the garlic until it goes golden brown. Add the anchovy fillets and cook until they dissolve. Throw in the spinach and wilt quickly, then set the pan aside.

In a large pan of boiling salted water cook the tagliatelle according to the instructions on the packet. Split the broccoli into fine pieces and, about 1 minute before the pasta is cooked, add to the pan with the pasta. Drain, reserving about 5 tablespoons of water.

Remove the bone from the veal rib and slice the veal into bite-sized pieces. Add these to the spinach and place the pan back on the heat. Add the pasta, broccoli and water. Toss everything together well and season. Finally add the lemon zest and juice and grate some Parmesan over the top.

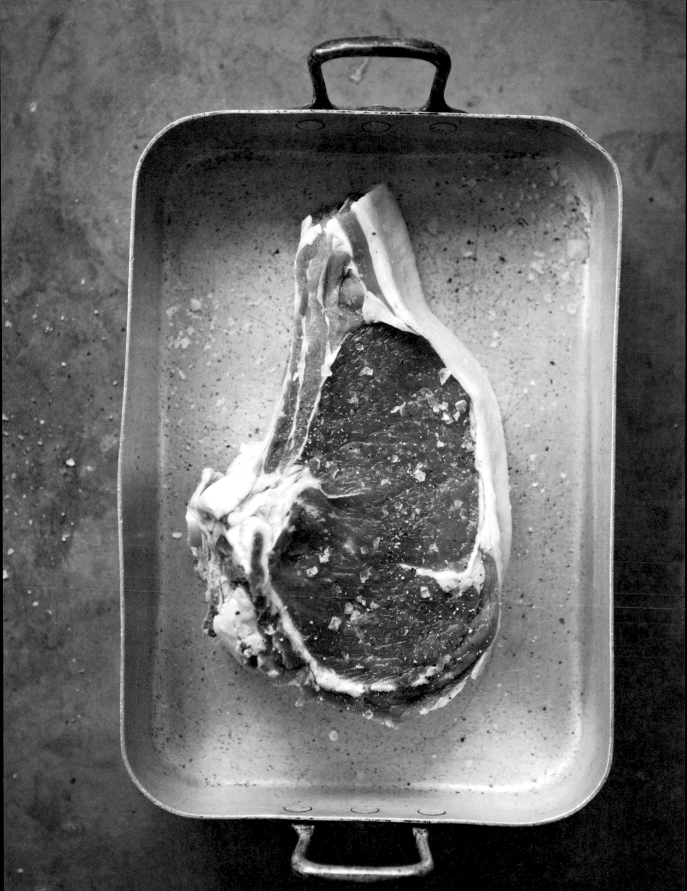

Glorious grouse 'David Pitchford'

SERVES 4

for the grouse

4 rashers of smoked streaky bacon, cut in half lengthways

4 grouse, cleaned, livers and hearts reserved for the pâté

sea salt and freshly ground black pepper

2 tbsp vegetable oil

110ml red wine

1 sprig of fresh thyme

1 bay leaf

500ml brown chicken stock (see page 238)

a bunch of watercress, to serve

for the pâté

110g salted butter

185g grouse livers and hearts (you could use chicken livers)

1 shallot, peeled and finely chopped

2 cloves of garlic, peeled and finely chopped

4 tsp cooking brandy

4 tsp ruby port

4 tsp Madeira

1 tsp fresh flat-leaf parsley, leaves only, chopped

1 tsp fresh tarragon, leaves only, chopped

4 slices of white bread

for the bread sauce

1 small onion, peeled

4 cloves

2 bay leaves

600ml whole milk

150g fresh white breadcrumbs

30g salted butter

I have come to look upon David Pitchford as a father figure – well, a father figure I get drunk and gamble with! He and his wife, Rona, run Read's Restaurant in Faversham and it was there that I had my first true taste of fine dining and, eventually, Michelin-star food. I can remember to this day the first time I set foot in his kitchen. I was seventeen years old and the sight of all the stockpots bubbling away and the sauces being made was incredible. David is old school but has a modern mentality and this really shines through in his food. It was this grouse dish that made me realize there was more to cooking than what we were being shown at college. The smell was like nothing I had ever encountered before and the bollocking I got for dipping my finger in the sauce was definitely worth it.

Preheat the oven to 220°C/gas mark 7.

First lay the bacon over the grouse breasts and secure them with kitchen string. Season the grouse well, inside and out. Heat the oil in an ovenproof frying pan over a high heat and fry, turning frequently, until the grouse is golden brown on all sides. Transfer to the oven for 10–12 minutes, until it is medium-rare, then remove the grouse from the pan and set aside on a warm plate to rest. Reserve the pan and any juices.

Heat the reserved pan that the grouse was cooked in over a medium heat and add the red wine, thyme and bay leaf to the pan juices. Stir well, scraping any browned bits off the bottom with a wooden spoon. Add the chicken stock and bring to the boil, then reduce the heat and simmer until the liquid has reduced by half. Season and strain the sauce through a fine sieve into a saucepan.

For the pâté, heat 2 tablespoons of the butter in a separate frying pan over a medium heat. When it is foaming, add the grouse livers and hearts and fry until golden brown on all sides but still pink in the centre. Add the shallot and garlic and fry for 1–2 minutes, until softened. Add the brandy, port and Madeira (measure them into one jug first to make this easier) and flambé quickly and carefully. When the flames have died down, add the parsley and tarragon to the pan and cook for 2–3 minutes, until heated through.

Season, then transfer the mixture to a food processor and blend to a smooth purée. Finally pass this through a fine sieve to remove any gristly bits. Cut the bread into four discs or, more traditionally, heart shapes. Heat the remaining butter in a separate frying pan over a medium heat and fry the bread until golden brown on both sides. Set aside to drain on kitchen paper.

For the bread sauce, stud the onion with the cloves and place it in a pan with the bay leaves and milk. Gently simmer the milk for 3–4 minutes, then allow it to stand for about 20 minutes to infuse. Strain the milk through a fine sieve into a clean pan and bring it back to the boil. Mix in the breadcrumbs and season. Heat the mixture over a medium heat, stirring occasionally, for 3–4 minutes, until thickened, then add the butter and whisk until melted.

To serve, spread the pâté over the croutons and place one on each of four serving plates. Remove the string from the grouse and push some of the watercress into the cavity, then place on top of a crouton. Serve the bread sauce and grouse gravy separately.

Roast pigeon 'Lord Nelson'

SERVES 4

4 oven-ready pigeons

4 sprigs of fresh thyme

4 cloves of garlic, whole and unpeeled

8 juniper berries

4 tbsp salted butter, plus extra for rubbing the bird

sea salt and freshly ground black pepper

4 tbsp olive oil

for the sprouts

675g Brussels sprouts, trimmed and cut in half

4 rashers of smoked streaky bacon, cut into lardons

75g fresh almonds (or dried if you can't get fresh)

10 prunes, pitted and cut into quarters

This is me being a bit silly, but if you think of Trafalgar Square filled with pigeons you will see where my idea came from. Horatio Nelson was born in Norfolk and the most famous bird from there is the Bronze turkey. Therefore I have chosen to give the pigeon a festive feel by adding some classic Christmas Day condiments, which go really well with the rich, plump bird.

Preheat the oven to 220°C/gas mark 7.

Stuff the pigeons with the thyme, garlic and juniper berries, then rub them over with butter and season well inside and out. Melt the butter and olive oil in a frying pan and, when the butter is foaming, add the pigeons, breast side down. Fry quickly, turning frequently, until well browned all over, then place the pigeons in a roasting tin and baste with the remaining pan juices. Transfer to the oven and roast for 12–15 minutes for a nice medium-rare. The pigeons should be firm to the touch with a slight bounce. Remove the birds and let them rest in a warm place.

Blanch the sprouts in boiling salted water for about 2–3 minutes, then plunge them into cold water to stop them cooking. Drain and dry on kitchen paper, then set aside. In a large frying pan cook the bacon until it is nice and crispy and has released all its fat. If you are using fresh almonds, add these to the fat and cook gently for 5 minutes; if you are using dried almonds, just sprinkle them in before adding the sprouts to the pan.

Season well and sauté for 5 minutes, or until the sprouts are warm and lightly browned. Throw in the prunes and stir them through, then transfer to a serving dish. Serve the sprouts alongside the pigeons, together with the Really Good Gravy (see page 242) if you like.

Underground veg

I wanted to split the vegetables into two chapters as there are so many delicious varieties they wouldn't all fit into one. Most vegetables that grow underground are roots, and plenty of them, such as carrots and parsnips, look like roots too. I know that onions grow half in and half out of the soil, but I'm not sure my publisher would appreciate a chapter called 'Half Below Half Above Veg'. I have tried to make most of the recipes substantial enough so that a combination would create a great vegetarian feast, but equally you can just mix and match them to go with the meat and fish recipes in the book.

Whole roast and spiced carrots

SERVES 4

8 medium carrots, the same size, peeled

1 sprig of fresh thyme

1 sprig of fresh rosemary

2 cloves of garlic, peeled and lightly crushed

2 star anise

3 cloves

1 bay leaf

sea salt

olive oil

a large knob of salted butter

Carrots are a versatile vegetable that can be cooked for a long time without breaking apart. This means they can be poached slowly with lots of flavourings, so they become lovely and soft but packed with flavour. Roasting them afterwards will give you a delicious golden-brown exterior as well. You'll never look at carrots the same way again.

Place the carrots, herbs and spices in a saucepan and just cover with water. Season well and bring to the boil. Simmer slowly for about 15–20 minutes, until the carrots are tender, then remove from the heat and allow them to cool in their cooking water.

When they have cooled, drain them carefully and pat dry with kitchen paper, then place them in the fridge for 20 minutes or so to chill completely. This allows the carrots to firm up again, meaning that you can fry them more easily, and is a perfect way to get them ready the day before a dinner party.

In a large frying pan heat some olive oil to just under smoking, then fry the carrots so they are golden brown all over. Turn the heat down, add the butter and roll the carrots around so they become lovely and glossy, then remove and serve. Plain carrots have just got wonderful.

Grilled honey-glazed turnips

You need nice big turnips for this recipe as you want to be able to see the beautiful criss-cross pattern left by the griddle pan. As with everything, use a good-quality honey. I'm lucky because my girlfriend's aunty has her own hives, so it's always Mottingham honey for me.

Preheat the oven to 200°C/gas mark 6.

Place the turnips in a saucepan and cover with cold water. Season with salt and bring to the boil. Simmer for 2 minutes, then drain and refresh under cold water. Pat dry with kitchen paper. Heat a griddle pan over a high heat until it is smoking hot, then drizzle the turnips with olive oil and place in the pan flat side down.

Cook for a few minutes, until the charred lines begin to appear, then give the turnips a quarter-turn and grill for a further few minutes. You should now have a charred criss-cross pattern. Put the turnip halves in an ovenproof dish with the criss-cross side up. Season and drizzle with honey, then bake in the oven for about 5–8 minutes, until they are lightly caramelized. Serve immediately.

SERVES 4

4 large turnips, peeled and cut in half
sea salt and freshly ground black pepper
olive oil
1 tbsp runny honey

Slow roast onions
with sherry vinegar

SERVES 4

olive oil

4 large white onions, left unpeeled and halved

1 head of garlic, left unpeeled and halved

sea salt and freshly ground black pepper

1 tbsp caster sugar

1 sprig of fresh thyme, leaves only

4 tbsp sherry vinegar

Onions contain lots of natural sugars and roasting brings out this sweetness, causing them to go a gorgeous golden brown. Sherry vinegar also has a sweet and sour flavour that goes really well with the browned onions.

Preheat the oven to 180°C/gas mark 4.

In a large non-stick pan heat some olive oil, then add the onions and garlic, cut side down, and fry until they are a lovely dark golden-brown colour. Remove to a plate and season well. Turn the heat down and sprinkle the pan with the caster sugar. When it is starting to caramelize, add the thyme and vinegar and bring to the boil, stirring until the sugar has dissolved.

Pour into an ovenproof dish just big enough to hold all the onions, then place the onions and garlic in, cut side down, so they are sitting in and soaking up the juices. Cover the dish with tin foil and bake for around 40–60 minutes, until the onions are lovely and soft and a deep golden brown. Turn them out on to a warm serving plate and eat straight from the skins.

Parsnip and cumin purée

SERVES 4

100g salted butter

500g parsnips, peeled and chopped into 2cm dice

1 tsp ground cumin

100ml double cream

sea salt

It's funny to think that the French hate this vegetable and usually feed it to horses. We clever Brits wised up a long time ago to the pleasures of parsnips. They make a fantastic thick and velvety purée, while cumin just enhances the flavour.

Melt the butter in a frying pan over a low heat and add the parsnips and cumin, then cover and cook slowly for about 25 minutes, until they are completely soft and falling apart. Add the cream and bring to the boil, then season, add 150ml water and liquidize to a smooth purée.

Baked celeriac in cream and garlic

Celeriac is a great vegetable and I love it. It has a light celery taste, as you might guess from the name, and is bright white and firm, so you can treat it almost like a potato. This is what I have done here, coming up with what's really a celeriac dauphinoise, but don't expect it to hold together like the potato version because celeriac doesn't contain starch.

Preheat the oven to 180°C/gas mark 4.

Grease a 1.2 litre oval ovenproof dish with butter and place a layer of celeriac slices on the base. Set aside a third of the cheese. Season the celeriac and sprinkle over a pinch of rosemary and a little cheese. Repeat layers of celeriac, rosemary and cheese until all the celeriac is used up.

In a small saucepan combine the cream, milk, garlic and bay leaf, bring to the boil and remove from the heat. Leave to infuse for about 10 minutes, then remove the bay leaf before pouring the cream mix over the celeriac, making sure that it filters all the way down to the bottom of the dish.

Sprinkle over a little grated nutmeg and top with the reserved cheese. Bake for about an hour, until the celeriac is tender and the sauce is bubbling and golden brown on top.

SERVES 4

butter, for greasing

1 celeriac, peeled (650g peeled weight) and thinly sliced

100g Emmental cheese, grated

sea salt and freshly ground black pepper

2 sprigs of fresh rosemary, leaves only, finely chopped

150ml double cream

50ml whole milk

2 cloves of garlic, peeled and crushed

1 bay leaf

freshly grated nutmeg

Hotpot potatoes

SERVES 4–6

2 tbsp olive oil

2 large onions, peeled (700g peeled weight) and thinly sliced

12 sprigs of fresh thyme, leaves only

sea salt and freshly ground black pepper

700g potatoes, such as Maris Piper, Desiree or King Edward

500ml white chicken (see page 239) or lamb stock

50g salted butter, softened

We have all enjoyed a nice lamb hotpot. Well, basically this is the same dish but without the lamb. You can use vegetable stock if you want to make it entirely vegetarian, but I prefer the flavour that a meat stock gives.

Preheat the oven to 190°C/gas mark 5.

Heat the oil in a medium pan and sweat the onions and thyme with some seasoning. Stir occasionally for 8–10 minutes, until the onions are soft and translucent. Peel and thinly slice the potatoes, preferably using a mandolin or the slicing attachment on a food processor.

Grease a wide, shallow ovenproof dish – it should be big enough to hold 1.2–1.5 litres – with a little oil, then arrange a quarter of the sliced potatoes on top. Sprinkle with salt and pepper, then scatter over a third of the onions.

Repeat layering the potatoes and onions, seasoning well in between and finishing with a top layer of potatoes. Bring the stock to the boil, then ladle it over the potatoes, letting it seep down the sides. You want the stock to reach only two-thirds up the sides of the potatoes and onions. Dot the top with the butter and bake for 45–50 minutes, until the potatoes are golden and crispy on top and soft and moist underneath.

Jacket sweet potato
with soured cream, chives and chilli

I am a relatively recent convert to the delights of butternut squash and sweet potatoes – I can't imagine why I never ate them before. I tried this recipe when I wanted a nice lunch but couldn't really be bothered to cook anything and it worked perfectly. The longer you leave these in the oven, the sweeter they become, so be patient – and make sure you use plenty of chilli to spice things up.

Preheat the oven to 200°C/gas mark 6.

Scrub the sweet potatoes clean, then prick them all over with a knife or fork. Cut four pieces of tin foil large enough to completely wrap each one and sprinkle a good pinch of salt in the middle. Sit each potato on top of a sheet of foil, drizzle with a little olive oil and wrap it up so there are no gaps. Bake in the oven for about 1 hour, or until the potatoes are lovely and soft.

Meanwhile, finely chop both chillies, leaving the seeds in if you like things hot. Tip the soured cream into a metal bowl and add the chillies, spring onions, chives, lime zest and juice and plenty of salt and pepper.

To serve, cut the potatoes in half and mash the middles up slightly, then drizzle a little sesame oil over each one and top with a good dollop of the soured cream mixture.

SERVES 4

4 medium-sized sweet potatoes

sea salt and freshly ground black pepper

olive oil

1 small red chilli

1 large green chilli

300ml full-fat soured cream

a bunch of spring onions, thinly sliced

a bunch of fresh chives, finely chopped

the zest and juice of 1 lime

a few drops of sesame oil

Crushed beetroot
with balsamic vinegar and butter

SERVES 4

2 tbsp olive oil

a large knob of salted butter

1 tsp coriander seeds

8–10 large cooked beetroot (750g), diced

3 tbsp good aged balsamic vinegar

½ bunch of fresh coriander, leaves only, chopped

sea salt and freshly ground black pepper

It is best to use fresh beetroot for this recipe and bake them first with plenty of sea salt to maximize the flavour. However, I will allow you to cheat and buy good-quality cooked beetroot if you have to, provided that you use a well-aged balsamic vinegar to make up for it!

In a large saucepan heat the olive oil and butter. When the butter begins to foam and sizzle, add the coriander seeds and fry gently for a minute or so to release the flavour. Add the diced beetroot and stir well. Start to crush the beetroot with a fork as it heats through, then add the balsamic vinegar and chopped coriander. Mix well and season, be generous with the pepper.

Salsify

roasted with sesame oil and soy

SERVES 4

600g salsify, washed, peeled and placed in a bowl of acidulated water (water to which a small amount of lemon juice or vinegar has been added to prevent discolouration)

sea salt

2 tbsp vegetable oil

1 tbsp runny honey

a large knob of salted butter

2 tbsp dark soy sauce

1 tbsp sesame oil

When I was a commis chef at Aubergine, working in the veg section, I vowed that I would never put salsify on the menu in my own restaurant as it was such a nightmare to prepare. Later, once I realized that it would no longer be me having to scrub the dirt off the long, strange-looking vegetable, I quickly changed my mind . . . after all, such things are character-building!

Remove the salsify from the acidulated water and place in a saucepan, then cover with cold water and season with salt. Place the pan over a high heat and bring to the boil quickly, as this helps stop the salsify from discolouring. Simmer for about 8 minutes, until the salsify is soft but still has a slight crunch to it.

Drain well, then cut into 5cm-long batons. In a large non-stick pan heat the vegetable oil until just smoking, then add the salsify and fry quickly to get a nice golden-brown colour on it. Add the honey and butter, cook for a further minute or so, then add the soy and sesame oil and reduce down to a syrupy glaze.

White radish
cooked with five spice and port

White radish, or mooli, is a formidable-looking vegetable and in its world size really does matter! When it is very fresh it has a mild flavour, being much less peppery than the little Breakfast radishes we are used to, so you need something to jazz it up. As it is used a lot in Asian cooking, I decided that the five spice powder would work really well, and the port adds a lovely ruby colour.

Place the white radish, five spice powder and salt in a large bowl, toss well and leave to steep for about 5 minutes, as the white radish will produce some moisture. Give things another toss and make sure that all the white radish is well coated in the five spice powder.

In a large frying pan heat the oil, then sauté the white radish until it is light brown all over. Doing this will also cook out the five spice powder and intensify the flavour. Pour in the port and simmer until the white radish is just tender, then turn up the heat and reduce quickly until you have a glossy red coating sauce. Serve immediately.

SERVES 4

1 medium (500g) white radish (mooli), peeled and cut into 2cm dice

2 tbsp five spice powder

sea salt

300ml tawny port

1 tbsp olive oil

Overground veg

There is something wonderful about vegetables that grow above the ground, sucking in fresh air and open to the elements. Take, for example, English asparagus. With its short season and premium price, it is prized much more highly than a new season carrot. Overground veg are also considered healthier than their underground cousins, because of the number of vitamins they contain, and I have heard cabbage described as the perfect food. However, the main thing is that they are delicious and I hope the recipes in this chapter do them justice.

Roast butternut squash

with rosemary, garlic and chilli

SERVES 4

**2 small butternut squash,
halved, deseeded and
roughly chopped**

**sea salt and freshly ground
black pepper**

**2 cloves of garlic, peeled and
crushed**

**1 red chilli, finely chopped and
deseeded**

**2 sprigs of fresh rosemary,
leaves only, finely chopped**

4 tbsp olive oil

This is great as a side dish or a vegetarian main
course and also works really well with pumpkin
or marrow. Use small, ripe squash with a vibrant
orange colour as they have a lovely natural
sweetness. This is a 'bung in the oven' dish that
gives impressive results and is perfect served in the
autumn with mixed roasted wild mushrooms.

Preheat the oven to 180°C/gas mark 4.

Place the squash chunks on a baking tray and score the flesh
using a small knife. Season well, then place in the oven for 10
minutes to kick-start the cooking process. In a bowl mix the
garlic, chilli, rosemary and oil and stir well to mash up all the
flavours.

Remove the squash from the oven and pour the flavoured oil
all over them, making sure every bit of squash is coated. Place
back in the oven for a further 30 minutes or so. Check halfway
through the cooking time and baste with any oil and juices that
are running. When the squash is soft and golden, remove from
the oven and serve.

Curly kale
with caramelized onions and anchovies

Kale is a vegetable that is slowly but surely becoming more popular and quite rightly so. By now you must have noticed that anchovies feature in a lot of my recipes, giving a depth of salty flavour that goes far beyond anything just adding salt can do. The sweet and sour onions work really well with the earthy, irony flavour of the kale, which is super-healthy too.

Cook the kale in lots of boiling salted water for 2–3 minutes, until it is soft with just a slight bite to it. Drain well and keep aside while you cook the onions. In a large frying pan heat the olive oil, then sauté the onions for about 10 minutes so they are nicely caramelized and golden brown.

When the onions are ready, add the anchovies and vinegar. Bring to the boil and stir so that the anchovies disintegrate and the vinegar evaporates. Add the kale to the pan and toss well to coat it all over with the sweet and sour, salty onions. Season and serve.

SERVES 4–6

200g curly kale, leaves removed and shredded

sea salt and freshly ground black pepper

2 tbsp olive oil

1 large onion, peeled and sliced

4 salted anchovies in oil, drained

4 tbsp sherry vinegar

Purple sprouting broccoli

with anchovy dressing

SERVES 4

400g purple sprouting broccoli

sea salt and freshly ground black pepper

1 clove of garlic, peeled

4 salted anchovies in oil, drained

1 tsp English mustard

2 tbsp red wine vinegar

6 tbsp olive oil

When this variety of broccoli is in season, you should definitely make the most of it. Not only does it have the best flavour, but in its raw state it looks beautiful. Sadly, the lovely purple colour is lost to the boiling water during cooking, but that doesn't matter when you taste it. Obviously you can eat this vegetable hot, but I prefer to have it at room temperature, smothered in this stunning dressing.

Cook the broccoli in boiling salted water for 3–4 minutes, until tender. Drain and allow to cool. Using a pestle and mortar, grind the garlic and anchovies with a little pinch of salt to a fine paste. Stir in the mustard and vinegar, then slowly add the oil so that it all emulsifies well.

Check the seasoning: it shouldn't need too much salt, but add plenty of black pepper. When it is at room temperature place the broccoli on a serving plate and coat it in the sharp and salty dressing.

English asparagus
with garlic and ginger butter

At six weeks, the season for English asparagus is unfairly short, but that just means you have to eat it as often as possible. It's grown all over the country and is delicious, but in my experience the best asparagus comes from East Anglia. You can add the same flavourings to a hollandaise sauce, but I prefer the warm, salty butter melted all over, as here.

Cook the asparagus spears in a large pan of boiling salted water until they are just tender with a very slight crunch. This should take no more than 3–4 minutes. Carefully remove them from the pan and drain well, then place on a serving dish and keep warm.

In a small pan melt the butter and add the garlic, ginger, lemon zest and juice, then season well. Keep stirring for a couple of minutes, to allow the flavours to infuse and to cook the ginger and garlic, before pouring the sauce over the asparagus.

SERVES 4

600g English asparagus, trimmed of the woody ends

100g salted butter

2 cloves of garlic, peeled and crushed

a small knob of fresh ginger, peeled and grated

the zest and juice of 1 lemon

sea salt and freshly ground black pepper

Sprouts
with lemon, sage and smoked bacon

SERVES 4

300g Brussels sprouts, trimmed

50g salted butter

125g smoked streaky bacon, cut into lardons

1 clove of garlic, peeled and crushed

2 tbsp fresh sage leaves, shredded

the zest of 1 lemon

sea salt and freshly ground black pepper

I love Brussels sprouts and simply can't understand why some people don't like them – apart from the memory of overboiled stinky, slimy mini-cabbages cooking in their nan's kitchen! The trick is to buy nice small sprouts that have had a frost and not to overcook them. Use a good smoked bacon, as it will make a big difference to the dish.

Cook the sprouts in salted boiling water for 3–4 minutes until just cooked, then drain and keep warm. Heat the butter in a large saucepan and fry the bacon for 2–3 minutes. Add the garlic and fry for a further minute, then add the sage leaves and lemon zest. Tip in the cooked sprouts and cook for 2–3 minutes, until the sprouts begin to colour, then season to taste and serve.

Pointed cabbage
in white wine and fennel seeds

SERVES 4–6

2 tbsp olive oil

1 tsp fennel seeds

1 large onion, peeled and sliced

1 large pointed cabbage, core removed and finely shredded

1 tbsp white wine vinegar

180ml dry white wine

sea salt and freshly ground black pepper

This is a variety of cabbage not really used that much any more, though I had it all the time at school. It is similar in texture to a white cabbage, which at school meant they would boil it for days . . . blurgh! However, that means it's suitable for braising and in this dish it is packed full of flavour. Use a fairly cheap dry white wine as you need some acidity – anything like a Chardonnay will not do the trick.

In a large saucepan heat a couple of tablespoons of olive oil, then add the fennel seeds and fry for a minute to release the flavour. Stir in the sliced onion and cook gently for a couple of minutes, then stir in the cabbage to coat in the oil and fennel seeds.

Pour in the vinegar and white wine, bring to the boil and allow to reduce by about half, then simmer on the stove for about 5 minutes until the cabbage is cooked and the sauce has thickened slightly. Season and serve.

Simple braised red cabbage

I have come across many versions of this recipe, some more complicated than others. Some people like to include apple; others add smoked bacon and onions. Some use port and red wine; others recommend sweating everything down with a bouquet garni and spices. Of all the recipes that I have tried, this is not only by far the best for bringing out the full flavour of the cabbage but is also super-easy. And yes, it is another great dish that I have stolen from David Pitchford – why deny it when the results are so tasty!

Preheat the oven to 180°C/gas mark 4.

Put the red cabbage in an ovenproof dish or pan, sprinkle over the sugar and vinegar and distribute the butter evenly. Season well, cover with a tight-fitting lid or tin foil and place in the oven.

Cook for 30 minutes, then give it a really good stir before putting it back for a further hour. By this time you will have a wonderful soft, glistening and aromatic cabbage dish to rival all others.

SERVES 4

1 red cabbage, core removed and shredded

250g demerara sugar

250ml malt vinegar

200g salted butter, diced

sea salt and freshly ground black pepper

Cauliflower
in tomato sauce

SERVES 4–6

50g salted butter

1 onion, peeled and finely chopped

2 bay leaves

1 sprig of fresh thyme

1 cauliflower, broken into florets

a pinch of dried chilli flakes

1 x 400g tin of chopped tomatoes

2 tbsp fresh flat-leaf parsley, leaves only, chopped

sea salt

I see the cauliflower as a thing of beauty, especially in early spring when, bright white and with tightly packed florets, it first comes into season. This is a great dish for those of you who want to try something with a bit more flavour than the standard cauliflower in a cheese sauce.

In a large saucepan melt the butter and add the onion, bay leaves and thyme. Cook for a few minutes until the onions are soft, then add the cauliflower and stir to coat it in butter. Add the chilli flakes and tomatoes, together with half a tin's worth of water.

Bring the liquid to the boil, then cover with a tight-fitting lid, turn down the heat and simmer for 10–12 minutes, until the cauliflower is tender. Check the contents of the pan: the cauliflower should be just soft and coated in a light tomato sauce. Sprinkle with parsley and season to taste before serving.

Baked courgettes
with olive oil and pink peppercorns

SERVES 4

4 large washed courgettes, cut in half lengthways

sea salt and freshly ground black pepper

2 tbsp pink peppercorns

5 tbsp olive oil

the zest and juice of 1 lemon

I must admit that I am not a massive fan of courgettes, but even I can manage them like this, so if you love courgettes this one will really appeal. Again, as with many of my recipes, it is quite simple but packed full of flavour. The pink peppercorns are a great addition, giving a spicy crunch and an almost Asian feel to the dish.

Preheat the oven to 180°C/gas mark 4.

Score the courgettes in a criss-cross pattern on the cut side, but be careful not to go all the way through. This will allow the flavours to seep into the courgettes. Place the courgettes on a baking tray, cut side up, and season well.

Using a pestle and mortar, grind the pink peppercorns coarsely – you don't want a fine powder – then mix in the olive oil and lemon zest and juice. Spoon this over the courgettes and bake them in the oven for 20–25 minutes, until tender. Remove to a serving plate and spoon over any juices that are left.

Marrow
with a parmesan crust

Marrow is the sort of vegetable that makes you feel quite nostalgic. It is the king of the allotment and the vegetable patch alike. My dad used to grow them at the end of the garden and we would have them every Sunday with our roast dinner for a time, then they just sort of disappeared from the dinner table. They are part of the same family as pumpkin and squash, so can be used in similar ways, but their flesh is softer, more like a courgette's, so don't overcook them.

Cut off the stalk, then peel the marrow, cut it in half lengthways and scoop out the seeds. Cut into 7cm cubes and wash these in cold water. Place them in boiling salted water, bring the water back to the boil, skim it and then simmer gently for 4–5 minutes.

Remove the marrow with a slotted spoon and drain well on a cloth. Put the marrow in a heatproof dish, then sprinkle the surface with the Parmesan, seasoning and butter. Glaze under a hot grill and serve.

SERVES 4

850g marrow

sea salt and freshly ground black pepper

50g Parmesan cheese, freshly grated

50g salted butter, melted

Sweet things

I wouldn't say that I have a massively sweet tooth really, preferring cheese after a meal rather than a pudding, but every now and then a spoonful of something sweet is just what the doctor ordered. My taste is generally light and citrus as opposed to rich and chocolatey, but I do stray on occasion. Here is a selection of rich, light and surprising puddings.

Ruby's bread pudding

Thick vanilla cream with drunken fruit

Caramel pastry with orange cream and marinated satsumas

Posh apple pie with walnut crumble

Fruit crumble meringue pie

Nanny Ada's rhubarb and custard

Passion fruit and banana tart

Melon and ginger jelly

Home-made yoghurt with Pedro Ximenez grapes

OK, a chocolate pudding!

Ruby's bread pudding

SERVES 6

50g unsalted butter, cut into small cubes, plus extra for greasing

300g stale bread (white or brown)

110g currants, raisins or sultanas (or a mix)

50g soft brown sugar

1–2 tsp mixed spice

2 large free-range eggs, beaten

approx. 200ml whole milk

icing sugar, sifted, to dust

There's not much to say about this recipe other than that it's from my late gran Ruby and is totally delicious. Also, it's a great way to use up stale bread, which we always seem to have, don't we?

Preheat the oven to 180°C/gas mark 4 and grease a 22 x 22 x 5cm ovenproof dish.

Break the bread into small pieces and soak in cold water for at least 1 hour. Strain and squeeze as dry as possible, then put it in a bowl and mash well with a fork. Add the dried fruit, sugar and mixed spice, making sure that you mix it well. Add the eggs and enough milk so the mixture drops easily from a spoon.

Tip into a greased ovenproof dish, dot the butter over the top and bake for 40–45 minutes, until slightly firm to the touch. When the bread pudding is done, turn it out on to a dish and dust with icing sugar. Either serve hot with lashings of custard or cream or – my favourite – allow to cool and spread with loads of salty butter.

Thick vanilla cream
with drunken fruit

SERVES 4

150ml whole milk

340ml double cream

1 vanilla pod, split in half

20g plain flour

15g cornflour

3 large free-range egg yolks

40g caster sugar

2 tbsp icing sugar, sifted

250–300g drunken fruit (see page 232)

Drunken Fruit (see page 232) get better the longer you leave them, so make up a batch as soon as you can and hold off eating them for as long as possible. Alternatively, you can buy the dried fruit listed there and just marinate them for a couple of hours. The cream is rich, thick and velvety and needs to be served nice and cold. This is really more of a winter pudding, but the cream goes well with summer fruit too.

Heat the milk, 100ml double cream and vanilla pod in a heavy-based saucepan until almost boiling. Sift the flour and cornflour together in a bowl. Beat the egg yolks and caster sugar together in another bowl, then tip the flour in and beat until smooth.

Add the hot creamy milk and whisk well until the mixture is smooth. Pour it back into the pan and whisk over a medium-low heat for 1–2 minutes, until thickened and smooth. Transfer to a bowl, cover and cool to room temperature, stirring occasionally to prevent a skin forming.

Whip the remaining double cream with the icing sugar to the soft-peak stage, then mix in the vanilla cream. Remove the vanilla pod and run your fingers down it to extract all the lovely little black seeds, which will add more flavour. Place in the fridge to chill for at least 30 minutes.

When the vanilla cream is nice and cold, spoon it into serving bowls and put the fruit over the top. Sometimes, if I fancy a quick burst of sweetness, I just pour some of the syrup from the fruit over the cream and leave it at that.

Caramel pastry
with orange cream and marinated satsumas

For me the pastry is the best bit of this recipe: it is buttery, sweet and crunchy all at the same time. You can now buy really good-quality brands of puff pastry, so there's no need to make it unless you really want to. You have to think ahead with the satsumas, as they should be marinated for the best flavour, but if you decide to use fresh fruit, that's just about OK!

Preheat the oven to 180°C/gas mark 4.

Roll out the pastry in neat 11cm squares to the thickness of a pound coin and let them rest in the fridge on a baking tray while you make the orange cream. Pour the cream into a bowl and whisk it until thickened slightly, then add the orange zest and icing sugar and whisk until it has firm peaks. Place the cream in the fridge and get the pastry out.

Brush the squares all over with egg wash and sprinkle them generously with the sugar. Bake in the oven until they are risen, golden brown and caramelized on the top, which should take about 20 minutes. Remove the pastry to a wire rack and allow to cool completely.

Place a pastry square in the centre of each plate and divide the cream between them, then break the marinated satsumas over the top. Drizzle with some of the marinating liquor and sprinkle with the mint.

SERVES 4

400g all-butter puff pastry
240ml double cream
the zest of 1 orange
2 tbsp icing sugar, sifted
1 large free-range egg, beaten
2 tbsp demerara sugar
4 marinated satsumas (see page 232)
6 large mint leaves, shredded

Posh apple pie
with walnut crumble

SERVES 6

4 Braeburn apples
50g caster sugar
50g unsalted butter
4 cloves
2 tbsp apple brandy
400g all-butter puff pastry

for the crumble topping
100g plain flour
75g cold unsalted butter
75g demerera sugar
50g chopped walnuts
a pinch of sea salt

There is no better pudding for me than a classic tarte Tatin, but I wanted to give it a British twist so have added the crumble. This dessert has it all: crisp, caramelized pastry with soft, sweet apples and a homely, nutty crumble topping. It also looks amaaaazing!

Heat the oven to 200°C/gas mark 6.

Core the apples, then peel them as neatly as possible and halve. Tip the sugar, butter and cloves into an ovenproof frying pan, about 20cm wide, and place over a high heat until bubbling and the sugar caramelizes to a toffee colour. Lay the apples in the pan and cook in the sauce for 10–12 minutes, tossing occasionally, until completely caramelized. Add the brandy and set it alight, then leave the apples to cool and absorb the caramel.

Roll out the pastry to the thickness of a pound coin. Using a plate slightly larger than the top of the pan, cut out a circle, then thin out the edges of the pastry by pressing them. When the apples have cooled slightly, arrange them in the pan, cut side up, in a neat pattern. Lay the pastry over the top, tucking the edges down the pan sides and under the fruit so the pastry is touching the caramel at the bottom of the pan – this will give you lovely crunchy pastry.

Pierce the pastry a few times, then bake for 15 minutes. Reduce the oven to 180°C/gas mark 4 and bake for a further 10–15 minutes, until the pastry is golden. Leave the tart to stand for 10 minutes while you make the crumble topping.

Mix all the crumble ingredients together lightly in a large bowl – you need nice lumps in there, so it goes lovely and crunchy in the oven. Tip the contents of the bowl on to a baking tray and cook in the oven at 180°C/gas mark 4 for 12–15 minutes, until it is golden brown. Carefully invert the apple tart on to a large serving plate and sprinkle with the crumble mix. You can serve it with cream, yoghurt or custard, but I like mine just as it is.

Fruit crumble meringue pie

This is a great recipe that combines two British classics to maximum effect. The brilliant thing about it is the way the soft creamy meringue acts as cream or custard would with your usual crumble, so it's an all-in-one dish. Change the fruit with the seasons and it's a year-round winner.

Preheat the oven to 180°C/gas mark 4 and grease a 22 x 22 x 5cm ovenproof dish.

To make the crumble, in a large bowl mix together the butter and the sugar using your fingertips until the mixture resembles breadcrumbs. Stir in the hazelnuts. Add the flour and mix until well combined. Scatter the mixture on a baking tray and bake for 10–15 minutes, until crisp and golden brown.

Meanwhile, chop the pears and place them in a saucepan with the sugar, star anise, lemon juice and 100ml water. Cook until just soft, but still with bite. Spoon the pears in an even layer on the greased dish. Measure out 50ml of the poaching liquor and pour over the pears. Sprinkle over the crumble mixture, bake for 10 minutes and set aside.

To make the meringue, put the sugar and 40ml water in a saucepan and slowly bring to the boil. Brush down the crystals on the sides of the pan with a clean brush dipped in cold water. Put a sugar thermometer in the pan and keep an eye on the temperature. you will need to add the sugar to the whisked egg whites once it reaches 120°C. Put the egg whites in a mixing bowl, add a tiny squeeze of lemon juice and whisk using an electric beater until firm peaks form when the whisk is removed.

Add the vanilla seeds when the whites are nearly stiff. Remove the sugar from the heat when it reaches 120°C. With the beater at its lowest speed, pour in the melted sugar in a steady stream, making sure it is clear of the beaters. Continue beating for about 5 minutes, until the meringue is tepid. Pipe the meringue over the crumble and finish by browning it with a mini-blowtorch or under a hot grill.

SERVES 6

for the crumble

110g cold unsalted butter, plus extra for greasing

110g demerara sugar

100g roasted hazelnuts, chopped

180g plain flour

for the filling

5 pears, peeled and cored

100g caster sugar

2 star anise

a squeeze of lemon juice

for the meringue

180g caster sugar

6 large free-range egg whites

a squeeze of lemon juice

1 vanilla pod, seeds only

Nanny Ada's rhubarb and custard

SERVES 4–6

500g rhubarb, trimmed and cut into chunks

the juice of 1 orange

2 tbsp golden caster sugar

for the custard

300ml double cream

1 vanilla pod, split

3 large free-range egg yolks

30g golden caster sugar

1 tbsp cornflour

150g crème fraîche

to serve

fresh mint sprigs

4 sponge fingers, crushed

I apologize for my slightly over-the-top nostalgia, but this is my very first book, so you will let me off, won't you? The fact is I'm just being honest about where my ideas and memories come from and this is a really strong one that I have from visits to my nan. I have obviously poshed this up quite a lot, but the flavour takes me straight back to her kitchen, which smelt of an old coal-burner and Grandad's kippers.

Put the rhubarb, orange juice and 2 tablespoons of golden caster sugar into a heavy-based saucepan and simmer until the rhubarb starts to break down. Remove from the pan and chill.

To make the custard, warm the cream with the split vanilla pod until small bubbles just begin to appear around the edges, then remove from the heat and set aside to cool a little. Beat the egg yolks, sugar and cornflour until creamy and pale, then pour in the lukewarm cream and whisk. Return the mixture to the saucepan and cook over a low heat until it boils gently and thickens. Pass through a sieve and chill.

Mix the cold custard and crème fraîche together until creamy, then gently fold in the rhubarb along with the liquor, saving some rhubarb for the top. Spoon the mixture into glasses and top with a little of the reserved rhubarb, then garnish with mint sprigs. Chill before serving and scatter over the crushed sponge biscuits at the last minute.

Passion fruit
and banana tart

Love it, love it, love it! You will be blown away by the flavour combinations in this pudding, as passion fruit and banana go together like tomato and basil or peaches and cream – it is one of life's perfect marriages. This makes a great birthday cake if you're bored of sponge or fruitcake.

Preheat the oven to 180°C/gas mark 4 and grease a 28cm tart case.

To make the pastry, place the flour, butter, salt and icing sugar in a food processor and pulse until it begins to look like breadcrumbs. Add the milk and egg yolks and pulse again until it comes together as a soft dough. Turn the dough out on to a floured work surface and roll to a diameter larger than the tart case. Push the pastry into the base of the tart case, leaving the excess hanging over the sides, and chill in the fridge for at least 30 minutes.

Line the chilled pastry case with tin foil and cover with rice or baking beans. Transfer to the oven to bake for 20 minutes, then remove the rice or beans and foil. Brush the pastry with the egg wash and return to the oven to bake for a further 10–15 minutes, until golden brown. Reduce the oven to 170°C/gas mark 3–4.

To make the filling, place 100g sugar, 75ml water and the passion fruit juice in a saucepan and heat gently until the sugar dissolves. Stir well, then remove from the heat and allow to cool. Whisk the eggs in a bowl with the remaining 125g sugar until pale and light, then pour in the cream and mix. Add the passion fruit syrup, reserving 3 tablespoons for the top. Pour the egg and cream mixture into the cooked tart case, then transfer to the oven to bake on the middle shelf for about 40 minutes, or until the filling has almost set. Remove and leave to cool for about 30 minutes, as it will continue to keep cooking.

To serve, peel and slice the bananas into 2cm rounds, then arrange them nicely on top of the tart. Spoon the remaining syrup on the top, together with some of the fresh pulp.

SERVES 6–8

for the pastry

225g plain flour, plus extra for dusting

75g cold unsalted butter, cut into cubes

a pinch of salt

100g icing sugar, sifted

50ml whole milk

2 large free-range egg yolks

1 large egg, beaten

for the filling

225g caster sugar

12 passion fruit, sieved to collect juice only, pulp reserved

4 large free-range eggs

150ml double cream

2–4 large ripe bananas

Melon and ginger jelly

SERVES 4

100g caster sugar

1 large, ripe Charentais melon

the zest and juice of 1 lime

a large knob of fresh ginger, peeled and grated

8g gelatine leaves (4–5 small sheets), soaked in cold water

This wonderful zingy summer dessert will freshen you up on the hottest day or reinvigorate your palate after the largest of meals. You can play around with different melons, as it works well with most of them, but my favourite would be a ripe, bright orange Charentais. It is naturally very sweet and its vibrant colour just looks so pretty. This jelly is made to sit in a glass or bowl, not to be turned out, as it is lightly set. I like a real kick to mine, so I add quite a bit of ginger juice, but try it as you go along and adjust according to taste.

First you need to make a stock syrup, so boil the sugar in 100ml water and when it is completely dissolved place it in the fridge to cool down. Meanwhile, cut the melon in half, remove the seeds and scoop out the flesh. Place in a blender with the lime zest and juice, purée until smooth, then add the cold stock syrup and purée again. (At this stage you could pass the mixture through muslin to get a really clear jelly, but I want more of a set purée to give you maximum flavour and texture.)

Place the grated ginger in a piece of muslin and over a bowl squeeze as hard as you can to extract the juice. You are going to use this to flavour the jelly. Add about half of the ginger juice to the melon purée and stir well, then taste to see if you think it needs more. I usually put it all in. Remove a small ladle of melon juice and warm it through in a saucepan, then squeeze out the gelatine and dissolve it in the warm juice. Add the gelatine mixture to the remaining melon juice and stir well. Pour into glasses or bowls and chill in the fridge until set (this will take at least two hours).

Home-made yoghurt
with Pedro Ximenez grapes

I've included a brilliant recipe for home-made yoghurt here but you could also just buy good-quality Greek yoghurt for this dish, because the real stars are the grapes. This was a purely accidental discovery on my part, as I had some seedless red grapes in the fridge that were getting a bit old and shrivelled and when I looked at them I just saw large sultanas. So, not to be wasteful, I put them on a tray in a very low oven and ended up with beautifully sweet grapes. Putting them in the sherry just made them extra good. And they are great with cheese too.

Pour the milk into a saucepan and warm on a medium heat, stirring gently, until it reaches 46°C. You can use a thermometer for this, but if you can just about hold your little finger in the milk without gritting your teeth it should be about right. Take the saucepan off the heat and pour the milk into a mixing bowl. Whisk in the yoghurt and blend well. Cover the bowl with a lid or cling film, then wrap in a towel and keep in a warm place like an airing cupboard or on top of a radiator. Leave the yoghurt for 6–8 hours. When it has thickened and set, it's ready to go in the fridge; if it's still a little runny, then just leave it a bit longer.

While the yoghurt is setting, preheat the oven to 110°C/gas mark ¼ and pick all the grapes off their stems. Place them on a clean non-stick tray and put in the oven. There is no set time for this, but after about 2 hours the grapes should start looking like large, soft sultanas. They should not be completely dry, more just soft shrivelled grapes. Once the grapes are ready, place them in a bowl, pour in the sherry and stir. Cover the bowl with cling film and place in the fridge to chill, stirring every now and then.

To serve, dollop the fresh yoghurt into a bowl and spoon over some of the grapes and juice.

SERVES 4

500ml whole milk

250g plain natural set yoghurt (must be made with live cultures)

500g seedless red grapes (preferably a few days old and just starting to dry out)

50ml Pedro Ximenez sherry

OK, a chocolate pudding!

SERVES 4

275ml single cream

a pinch of dry chilli flakes

200g dark chocolate (minimum 70% cocoa solids)

2 large free-range egg yolks

3 tbsp whisky (I use Laphroaig as it has a wonderful flavour)

20g salted butter

The reason for the name is that I was told every cookery book must have something chocolatey in it, even though I wasn't keen. Don't get me wrong, I love the odd square of bitter chocolate or a couple of rich truffles with my coffee at the end of a meal, but chocolate puddings are not my favourite. However, this rich, velvety little number is something special. It should satisfy any chocoholic's lust and has a bit of a kick to it as well.

Heat the cream with the chilli flakes for a few minutes without allowing it to boil, then strain into a clean pan to remove the chilli. Break the chocolate into chunks, add them to the cream and melt over a low heat, stirring all the time to combine the two ingredients to a smooth, velvety consistency.

Remove from the heat and allow to cool slightly before adding the egg yolks and whisky. Beat lightly to combine. Once the mixture has cooled slightly, stir in the butter until it has completely melted and is well blended. Pour into ramekins and refrigerate for a couple of hours before serving.

Savoury things

Now you're talking! If I had a real man's appetite, I would always finish off my meals with a savoury, just like the fine diners of the past. As I mentioned earlier, my sweet tooth doesn't come out that often and I much prefer to end with something salty, so these recipes are just the ticket. For the most part, the savoury course has disappeared from menus, but thankfully there are still some great restaurants that keep the tradition going. It's true that for health reasons people tend to eat fewer courses now, which might explain why the savoury has lost its place, but every once in a while you could treat yourself – or just have one on its own for lunch.

- Scotch woodcock

- Home-made crumpets with marmite and poached egg

- Gruyère and paprika pastry straws

- Canapé Boodle's

- Oysters on toast with oyster sauce

- Flat-cap mushrooms with Cheddar and mushroom ketchup

- Sautéed cockles on garlic bread

- Garlic herring roes on toast

- Boiled duck egg with anchovy soldiers

- Roast garlic purée on toasted muffin

Scotch woodcock

SERVES 4

4 large slices of wholemeal
  bread
soft salted butter
Gentleman's Relish or anchovy
  paste
6 tbsp whole milk
6 large free-range eggs
a pinch of cayenne pepper
1 x 50g tin of salted anchovies
  in oil, drained

It's important to make your eggs nice and creamy
for this dish and the toast should be hot and well
buttered. As with all my recipes, using the best eggs
is a must and I always recommend Burford Browns.

Toast the bread, remove the crusts (of course) and spread with
butter. Cut in half and spread with Gentleman's Relish. Melt a
knob of butter in a saucepan. In a small bowl, whisk together
the milk, eggs and cayenne pepper, then pour into the pan
and stir slowly over a gentle heat until the mixture begins to
thicken. Remove from the heat and stir until creamy. Divide the
mixture between the anchovy toasts and top with thin strips of
anchovy fillet, arranged in a criss-cross pattern.

Home-made crumpets
with marmite and poached egg

Savouries are not just all about fine dining. This is a great dish to have for tea and something I would have eaten on a Sunday night before bed as a kid. Obviously the crumpets would have been from a shop, but it is really easy to make them and fun for children to watch as they bubble up. If you hate Marmite you can leave it out, but if you're anything like me you will put loads on! I will also share a secret with you: you can now get Marmite XO, which is mind-blowingly tasty.

Grease 4 crumpet rings or 7.5cm plain pastry cutters.

Place the flour and salt in a large bowl and stir in the sugar and yeast, making a well in the centre. Pour in the warm milk and water and mix to give quite a thick batter. Beat well until completely combined and cover with a tea towel or cling film. Leave in a warm place to rise for about an hour, until it's a light, spongy texture. Stir well to knock out any air and pour into a large jug.

Heat a non-stick frying pan over a very low heat with a drop of oil, then wipe the pan with kitchen paper to remove any excess – you only need the pan to be covered by a very thin film of oil. Sit the greased crumpet rings in the pan and leave to heat up for a couple of minutes before pouring in enough mixture to fill the rings just over halfway up the sides. Leave to cook until plenty of small holes appear on the surface and the batter has just dried out. This will take about 8–10 minutes.

Remove the rings and turn over the crumpets to cook for a further 1–2 minutes on the other side. When you have made your crumpets, butter them well and spread a thick layer of Marmite over them. Reheat your poached eggs in hot water for two minutes, drain and pat dry, then season well with pepper. Place an egg on each crumpet and serve.

* Makes 16 crumpets – the leftover mixture freezes well.

SERVES 4*

450g plain flour, sifted
½ tsp salt
1 tsp sugar
1 x 7g sachet fast-action dried yeast
300ml warm whole milk
300ml tepid water
olive oil
soft salted butter
lashings of Marmite
4 large free-range eggs, poached
freshly ground black pepper

Gruyère and paprika pastry straws

MAKES APPROX. 28

200g block of all-butter puff pastry

100g Gruyère cheese, finely grated

1 tbsp sweet smoked paprika

1 small free-range egg, beaten

2 tbsp freshly grated Parmesan cheese

flour for dusting

If you have any leftover puff pastry then this recipe is perfect. Lots of cheese and lots of smoky paprika make these seriously moreish.

Preheat the oven to 180°C/gas mark 4.

Roll out the pastry to about 16mm thick on a lightly floured surface. Scatter over a third of the Gruyère and sprinkle a third of the paprika evenly over that, then roll them firmly into the pastry. Fold the pastry in half and roll out again to about the same thickness.

Repeat the process twice more with the other thirds of the Gruyère and paprika, then roll out for the last time to about 2mm thick to make a rectangle measuring 28 x 18cm. Brush with the beaten egg and sprinkle over the Parmesan and leave to rest in the fridge for 30 minutes. Cut the pastry into strips about 1cm wide and 18cm long. Take each strip of pastry and twist each end in opposite directions until the whole strip is completely and evenly twisted, then lay them on a non-stick baking tray.

Bake for 8–10 minutes, until they are golden brown, puffed up and crisp. Remove from the oven and leave to cool slightly, as they are best eaten warm.

Canapé Boodle's

SERVES 2

4 thick slices of white bread

8 small flat mushrooms, peeled and stalks removed

sea salt and freshly ground black pepper

60g salted butter

4 rashers of good-quality back bacon

8 tbsp Welsh rabbit (see below)

for the Welsh rabbit

50g unsalted butter

50g plain flour

200ml whole milk, brought to the boil

100g mature Cheddar cheese, grated

3 tbsp Lea & Perrins

1 tsp English mustard

130ml Guinness

2 large free-range egg yolks

100ml whipped cream

This is a great savoury from my time working at Boodle's. Sadly, these days you will generally find a savoury course only in such stalwart places as gentlemen's clubs and some of the older restaurants, like Rules in London. Which is obviously a shame, as it's a wonderful way to end a meal if you can fit it in.

Toast the bread and trim off the crusts, then cut the slices in half. Season the mushrooms, put a knob of butter on each one, then place them on a baking tray and grill until cooked through. Next grill the bacon rashers on both sides until they are crispy.

For the Welsh rabbit, in a saucepan melt the butter, add the flour, cooking briefly, then add the hot milk a little at a time, stirring continuously to form a smooth sauce. Add the grated cheese and mix well, then add the Lea & Perrins and English mustard to taste. In another pan boil the Guinness to a syrup so it reduces to 1 tablespoon, then stir into the cheese mixture.

Cool down, then mix in the egg yolks and fold in the whipped cream. Place two mushrooms on top of each piece of toast and then a rasher of bacon. Spoon a couple of tablespoons of the rabbit mix over and grill until light brown.

Oysters on toast
with oyster sauce

This one makes sense, doesn't it? Oysters with oyster sauce – how can you go wrong?

Toast and butter the bread, remove the crusts, then set it aside and keep warm. Carefully open the oysters, saving the juices, and place in a saucepan. Strain the juices back over to remove any shell (you'll get about 2 tablespoons). Warm gently over a medium heat until the oysters begin to firm up, then carefully stir in the oyster sauce. When the oysters are coated in the sauce, divide them between the toast and serve.

SERVES 4

4 slices of sourdough bread
soft salted butter
12 large oysters
2 tbsp oyster sauce

Flat-cap mushrooms
with Cheddar and mushroom ketchup

SERVES 4

olive oil for frying

4 large flat-cap mushrooms, peeled and stalks removed

2 tbsp mushroom ketchup

freshly ground black pepper

100g Cheddar cheese, grated

Mushroom ketchup is a bit like Lea & Perrins but has a lovely sour flavour. Flat caps are my favourite mushrooms next to ceps, believe it or not, as they have such a gorgeous meaty flavour and texture. Please use a good strong Cheddar for this – I would recommend Montgomery.

Set the grill to its highest setting. In a large pan heat the olive oil, then fry the mushrooms for 3 minutes on each side. When they are almost cooked, add the mushroom ketchup and sizzle until it has all been absorbed.

Place the mushrooms, stalk side up, on a baking tray and season with pepper. Divide the cheese between the mushrooms and heat under the grill until golden brown and bubbling. Eat as they are or with bread and butter.

Sautéed cockles on garlic bread

SERVES 4

4 thick slices of French bread

olive oil

50g salted butter

2 cloves of garlic, peeled and crushed

½ bunch of fresh flat-leaf parsley, leaves only, chopped

300g cooked and picked cockles

sea salt and freshly ground black pepper

Cockles are an old East End classic. They are, to my mind, a little bit like snails, so I treat them the same way in this recipe. Lots and lots of garlic and parsley on soft but crunchy bread makes for a superb savoury – but you'll be going home alone if you eat this one!

Place a griddle pan on a high heat. Drizzle the French bread with olive oil. When the pan is smoking hot, add the bread and griddle on both sides until nicely charred. Remove and keep warm.

In a large frying pan melt the butter and when it foams throw in the garlic. Cook until it just starts to brown slightly, then add the parsley and the cockles. Stir for a couple of minutes to warm the cockles through, season, then spoon them over the bread and serve.

Garlic herring roes on toast

I have to admit that soft herring roes, or milts as they are otherwise known, are not everyone's cup of tea. But if fresh and cooked properly, they are truly delicious, so don't be put off by their raw state.

Season the flour well with salt and pepper before lightly dusting the roes in it. Heat the oil and butter in a large frying pan over a medium heat and add the garlic. When the garlic is lightly toasted and has imparted its flavour, add the roes and let them sizzle gently for 5–6 minutes, turning them over halfway through the cooking time, until they develop a golden-brown crust.

Meanwhile, toast and butter your bread. Sprinkle the parsley over the roes, then serve them piping hot from the pan on toast, with the halved lemons on the side.

SERVES 4

12–16 fresh soft herring roes

50g plain flour

sea salt and freshly ground black pepper

1 tbsp rapeseed oil

a small knob of salted butter, plus extra for buttering

1 clove of garlic, peeled and crushed

4 slices of granary bread

1 tbsp fresh flat-leaf parsley, leaves only, chopped

2 lemons, halved

Boiled duck egg
with anchovy soldiers

SERVES 4

4 free-range duck eggs

1 tbsp tapenade

10 salted anchovies in oil,
   drained and finely chopped

4 pieces of sliced white bread
   (the cheaper the better for
   this recipe)

olive oil for frying

My favourite anchovies rear their beautiful heads again in this dish. They are perfect for savouries, as they have a lovely salty flavour. Here they are deliciously sandwiched between two slices of bread to dip into soft, rich egg yolks.

Carefully place the eggs in a pan of boiling water and cook for 6–7 minutes. Meanwhile, in a small bowl mash together the tapenade and anchovies so that they form a rough paste. Spread this over the bread slices, then sandwich them together so you have two pieces of bread.

Flatten them with a rolling pin to make sure they stick together. Heat some oil in a large non-stick pan and fry the bread until golden and crisp on both sides. Remove the crusts and cut into soldiers. Place the eggs in eggcups and dip in your salty soldiers to your heart's content.

Roast garlic purée on toasted muffin

Large bulbs of fresh garlic make a wonderful sweet purée when slowly roasted in the oven. The roasting takes away any of the harsh, bitter flavour that garlic can have, leaving you with a soft, creamy and aromatic spread that is totally delicious.

Preheat the oven to 160°C/gas mark 3.

Place the cloves of garlic in an ovenproof dish and season with salt. Scatter over the thyme and rosemary, then drizzle with a little olive oil. Rub the garlic all over with your hands to make sure the seasoning and herbs are well mixed.

Cover the dish with foil and bake in the oven for about 1 hour, until the cloves are really soft. If you think the garlic is roasting too quickly turn the oven down slightly – you don't want it too brown or it will be bitter.

Once cooked and cool enough to handle, pop the sweet cloves from their skins into a bowl and strain any juices from the dish over them. Then take a fork or spoon and crush them to a purée. This is now ready to spread on whatever you like – personally I love a lightly toasted muffin. You can keep any spare purée in the fridge for a couple of days, but make sure it's well-sealed so the fridge doesn't smell.

SERVES 4

6 heads of garlic, broken into cloves and unpeeled

sea salt

1 sprig of fresh thyme

1 sprig of fresh rosemary

olive oil

4 muffins

Back to basics

My list of basics is slightly different from those in other books. Most of the recipes here will keep well and indeed get better with age, allowing you to dip in and out and use them when you want. They are home-made store cupboard ingredients and most of the hard work is simply waiting for them to be ready! I have also included a few of the stocks, as no basics list would be complete without them, plus my favourite gravy recipe, as I do tend to make these in my own special way.

Drunken fruit

1 packet each of dried prunes, dried apricots and dried figs

1 bottle of brandy (cooking brandy is fine)

2 cinnamon sticks

5 star anise

10 cloves

Effectively this recipe is just lots of dried fruits steeped in lots of booze. Be careful, as it has the potential to blow your head off.

Empty the fruit into a large bowl and add the brandy and spices. Mix really well to make sure the fruit is well covered, then transfer to a sealable jar or plastic bucket with a lid. Push the fruit down and top up with more brandy if necessary – it needs to remain submerged. Seal and leave to steep for at least a month.

Marinated satsumas

10 satsumas

2 cinnamon sticks

1 vanilla pod, split in half

1 bottle of Amaretto

Great to make ahead in time for Christmas – yet another excuse to include alcohol in your Xmas feast.

Carefully peel the satsumas so they remain whole and place them in a suitable jar for storing. Add the cinnamon sticks and vanilla, then pour over the Amaretto so that it completely covers the fruit. If it doesn't, then top up with boiling water, but you shouldn't need too much. Seal and store for at least 2 weeks, or longer if you can.

Preserved lemons

16 lemons

150g sea salt

These are perfect for adding a Middle Eastern touch to things like rice or couscous. They are less salty than the ones you can buy.

Wash the lemons in warm water and pat dry. Cut them in half and squeeze the juice into a jug or bowl. Place the lemons in a separate bowl and mix well with the salt, making sure that you really rub it in. Push the lemons into your chosen storage jar, then pour over the juice. If the juice doesn't completely cover the lemons, then top up with boiling water. Seal and turn the jars around a bit. Turn the jars a few times every day to help the salt dissolve – eventually it will vanish completely.

Home-made salami/chorizo

1kg roughly minced pork shoulder

200g diced or minced pork back fat

25g salt

1 clove of garlic, peeled and crushed

1 tsp fennel seeds

1 tsp crushed black pepper

1 tsp smoked or plain paprika

1 tsp cayenne pepper

½ glass of red wine

natural sausage skins (ask your butcher)

A trip to River Cottage a few years ago inspired me greatly and Hugh F-W is what I would call a real foodie, if not totally barmy. It was there that I got the home-cured meat bug and have been hooked ever since.

In a large bowl mix all the ingredients (except the sausage skins, obviously) together really well, as you want to make sure that the flavourings and especially the salt are evenly distributed. Rinse the sausage skins in plenty of cold water and leave to soak for 30 minutes. Place the mixture in a sausage machine or piping bag with a sausage nozzle. Pipe the sausages to the required size and tie off with string.

Prick any bubbles with a wooden toothpick to expel little air pockets which will cause the salamis to burst. Hang in a cool place with a little humidity, like a basement or a shed, to air-dry for about a month. The salamis should lose about 30 per cent of their original weight. I'm told they should keep a few months, but I've always eaten them too quickly to find out.

The first few attempts may not turn out quite as you had hoped, as getting the right drying location is key here, but this is all part of the fun to my mind. I would suggest making these in the cooler months, as they tend to dry out too much in the summer. This is very much a home version but it does give you good results. To switch from salami to chorizo, just use smoked paprika instead of plain.

Home-cured bacon

This is me going on about the Good Life again, but when you are slicing your own dry-cured bacon after just a few weeks, you will understand why. It really is very easy, and should you have a wood-burning fire, you can place it in the chimney breast overnight to smoke in the embers and it will be even nicer.

1kg coarse salt
6 bay leaves, shredded
20 juniper berries, crushed
200g soft brown sugar
25g crushed black pepper
1 whole pork belly, bone in (approx 2.5–3kg)
malt vinegar

Mix all the dry ingredients together in a plastic container. Rub the pork belly all over with malt vinegar to clean it of any bacteria, then lay it in a plastic tray and rub the salt mix generously over both sides. Place the tray in a cool place and tilt it so that any liquid runs away. After one day there will be a brown pool that needs to be drained off. Rub the pork belly again with more salt mix and repeat this every day until the salt has been used.

Leave to marinate in the salt mix for 10 days, draining the liquid as it comes out. Then remove the pork belly and rinse well in cold water to remove the excess salt. Pat dry with a clean cloth and rub over once again with vinegar. At this stage the pork belly can be smoked or more spices can be added, such as crushed peppercorns on the bone side. Wrap in clean muslin and hang in a cool place for a minimum of 1 week, but longer if you want firmer, dryer bacon; 3 weeks would be ideal.

This really is a wonderful way to eat your own bacon and, bearing in mind that you can probably get a whole pork belly for around £12, that's a lot of bacon for not much money!

English mustard mayonnaise

MAKES APPROX. 400ML

1 tbsp English mustard

2 medium free-range egg yolks

4 tbsp cider vinegar

4 salted anchovies in oil, drained

200ml vegetable oil

200ml olive oil

a good squeeze of lemon juice

sea salt

This is a very simple recipe that people often get so wrong. Lots of recipes call for Dijon mustard, but I like to use English – and lots of it – to get a great flavour.

Put the mustard, egg yolks, vinegar and anchovies in a food processor and give everything a good blitz. Scrape down the sides of the bowl, then turn the processor back on and this time slowly drizzle in the vegetable oil. You need to start really slowly at first, but as the mixture starts to emulsify you can pour it in a bit faster.

Once all the vegetable oil has been added, you may need to add a teaspoon of hot water just to loosen it slightly so that you can add the olive oil. Once all the olive oil has been added, then squeeze in the lemon juice and season with sea salt. You should end up with a lovely thick and flavoursome mayonnaise. You can keep any spare in the fridge for a few days.

Brown chicken stock

2kg chicken wings

olive oil

1 large leek, chopped

1 large carrot, peeled and chopped

1 large onion, peeled and chopped

2 sticks of celery, chopped

3 cloves of garlic, peeled and halved

1 large spoon of tomato purée

1 small spoon of chicken bouillon powder

1 glass of white wine

2 bay leaves

1 large sprig of fresh thyme

10 black peppercorns

10 coriander seeds

1 pig's trotter, cut in half lengthways

sea salt

Even when working in a professional kitchen I stopped making veal stock a long time ago, as I find it flavourless, expensive and it takes for ever. Instead I prefer to make brown chicken stock, to which I add a pig's trotter for the gelatine. This light stock, which tastes delicious on its own, is also a fantastic base for stews and brown sauces.

Preheat the oven to 200°C/gas mark 6.

Place the chicken wings in a roasting tray and drizzle with a little olive oil, then roast them for about 40–50 minutes, stirring occasionally, until they are lovely and golden brown. Transfer the chicken to a colander to drain, then place the leek, carrot, onion, celery and garlic in the roasting tray with another splash of oil if needed.

Roast for about 30 minutes, until they are nicely browned, then add to the colander to drain. Put the roasting tray on the stove over a high heat, add the tomato purée and stir quickly for about a minute. This cooks out the bitter taste of the purée. Add the bouillon powder and wine and reduce rapidly, scrapping up all the sediment in the pan.

Transfer the chicken, vegetables and the pan juices to a large pot. Cover with cold water, then add the bay leaves, thyme, peppercorns, coriander seeds and pig's trotter. Season with salt, bring to the boil, skim and simmer for 4 hours, removing any scum that forms and topping up with water if necessary.

When the time is up, pass the stock carefully through a muslin-lined colander and leave to settle. It is now ready to use. When it cools the stock will set like a jelly because of the pig's trotter and this is what will give a wonderful shine to your sauces.

White chicken stock

The base for most good soups and sauces, this can be delicious on its own in a mug if made properly. I use chicken wings, as they give a really good strong chicken flavour. Of course, you could use chicken carcasses, but in writing this recipe I am thinking of you making it for a specific reason and not just to use leftover bones. There is a very good reason why this is known as Jewish penicillin!

Place the chicken wings in a large pan, cover with cold water, then put over a high heat and bring to the boil. Skim really well as any scum rises to the top and continue this for about 20 minutes, until the stock is clear. Put the rest of the ingredients into the pan with the chicken. A good pinch of sea salt really brings out the flavour of the stock.

Bring back to the boil and simmer very gently for 3 hours, skimming whenever needed. By this time your stock should have a real depth of flavour. Place a muslin-lined colander over a large bowl and carefully strain the stock. It is now ready for use.

2kg chicken wings

1 large leek, chopped

1 large carrot, peeled and chopped

1 large onion, peeled and chopped

2 sticks of celery, chopped

2 bay leaves

1 large sprig of fresh thyme

3 cloves of garlic, peeled and halved

10 white peppercorns

10 coriander seeds

1 small spoon of chicken bouillon powder

sea salt

Vegetable stock

MAKES 1.5 LITRES

3 onions, peeled and chopped

1 leek, chopped

2 sticks of celery, chopped

6 carrots, peeled and chopped

1 head of garlic, cut in half, cloves left unpeeled

1 lemon, cut into 6 wedges

¼ tsp white peppercorns

1 bay leaf

4 star anise

200ml dry white wine

1 sprig each of fresh tarragon, basil, coriander, thyme, parsley and chervil

This stock is useful for all sorts of things. A good replacement for white chicken stock if you are a vegetarian, it is a great base in its own right.

Place all the ingredients except the wine and fresh herbs in a large pan, add 2 litres of cold water and bring to the boil. Simmer for 10 minutes, then remove from the heat. Add the wine and herbs, making sure that they are submerged, and leave to cool. Transfer to a bowl, cover and keep cool for 24 hours. Strain through a fine sieve and store in a clean jar or container.

A really good gravy

1 heaped dsp plain flour

1 glass of white wine

1 litre vegetable or chicken stock, either bought or home-made (see pages 238–40)

1 tbsp Lea & Perrins

1 tbsp tomato ketchup

1 tbsp HP Sauce

sea salt and freshly ground black pepper

This is my method for making gravy that will go with any roast. Although the ingredients are the same, the pan juices from the different roasts will change the flavour each time you make it. It's a real winner.

Place your roasting tray on the hob over a medium heat and let it sizzle a bit, then sprinkle in the flour. Stir well, making sure that it gets nice and brown and soaks up all the fat and juices. Add the wine, then stir vigorously to stop any lumps forming. Let this bubble a bit before adding the stock.

Turn up the heat to achieve a rapid boil, then, when the stock is bubbling away, add the Lea & Perrins, ketchup and HP Sauce. Whisk them in, season and, once you have a glossy gravy, strain it through a sieve into a jug. Stir any resting juices into the gravy and serve immediately.

Index

Page numbers in **bold** denotes an illustration

Acknowledgements

It takes a lot of people to work on a book like this and make it special, and believe it or not it's not all about me! The words written here don't really do justice for how much appreciation I have for the following people, but there is only a certain amount of space left in the book to get a little gratitude in print.

Firstly this book would not have come about if it wasn't for Felicity Blunt, my agent from Curtis Brown, who managed to persuade the publishers to take a leap of faith and get my first ever solo book in print.

The publisher brave enough to take on this responsibility was Richard Milner, together with David North and Caroline Proud. I'd also like to thank Josh Ireland and all the team at Quercus. I am their first ever chef, so I hope I do them proud. Thank you for your trust and I hope we work together for many years to come.

I'm grateful to Sarah Fairburn of Ian Fleming Publications, and the Fleming Estate, for granting permission to reproduce the brilliant James Bond scrambled eggs recipe.

Whilst I have cooked every dish for the stunning pictures in this book, it takes a real talent to make them look amazing. This talent belongs to the two Emmas: Emma Lee for her incredible eye and vision for the book, and Emma Thomas for the brilliant styling. I must also thank them for putting up with my dreadful sense of humor, which must have made their days longer than they had planned!

A big thank you to Simon Dyer, my head chef from Rocksalt, who gathered ingredients and worked very hard behind the scenes to help me with the styling. He was very proud that his mussels dish made the finished shot.

To make sure that my recipes work took a lot of time and effort, so huge thanks go to Lisa Harrison and her helpers Anna Burges-Lumsden and Lucinda Kaizik for spending hours in their kitchens cooking, adjusting and taking photos of my food.

A huge thank you goes to Michael Eyre and Martin Beesley from Jestic, who let me foolishly into their demonstration kitchen to cook the food for the photo shoots. I had nowhere to do this and they came to my aid without hesitation. I had lots of fun playing with the Josper.

Mike the Cheese from Drings Butchers in Greenwich was a huge source of inspiration to me, and gave me a few of his secrets to use in this book. Not enough though!

I would also like to thank Keith Chapman and David Theze from Chapman's of Sevenoaks for supplying me with the freshest fish, all at the last minute. I have never seen more lively whelks.

Big kiss goes to my Mum. Your support and encouragement got me where I am!

As they say I have saved the best until last, so a very big thanks and huge love goes to Nancy and Ivy. Constant support, loyalty and belief do not go unnoticed. I hope you enjoyed eating all my dishes as I was coming up with them. Now get down the gym!!